Advance Praise fc  D0289545

The Power of Self Management

"*The Power of Self Management* gives employees the information, tools and inspiration needed to effectively manage their work life, their behavior, and effectively deal with real work challenges."

Sandi Dornhecker
Vice President of Human Resources

"...loaded with practical ideas and no-nonsense recommendations to achieve job success and satisfaction."

Barbara Thomas
Corporate Manager of Education Services

"...a terrific tool to help employees successfully address conflicts with customers, boss and co-workers."

Lorraine Harris
Director of Human Resources

"...puts the power in the hands of the individual by providing practical scenarios, solutions, check lists and exercises."

Michelle Cooney
First Vice President of Learning and Development

"...a wonderful starting point for engaging in difficult discussions. It helps the reader get grounded and motivated to make responsible decisions."

Marbet Cuthbert
AVP of HR and Administration

THE
POWER
OF SELF
MANAGEMENT

Pride and Professionalism for a Successful Career

MICHAEL HENRY COHEN

CREATIVE

HEALTH CARE

MANAGEMENT

ISBN 13: 978-1-886624-81-8

Cohen, Michael Henry.
THE POWER OF SELF MANAGEMENT : PRIDE AND PROFESSIONALISM FOR A SUCCESSFUL CAREER / by Michael Henry Cohen.
    p. cm.
Includes bibliographical references.
ISBN: 978-1-886624-81-8 (pbk. : alk. paper)
    1. Employees—Attitudes. 2. Self-management (Psychology). I. Title.
HF5548.8.C568 2008
650.1—dc22

Printed and bound in the United States of America

Second Printing: December 2008

13 12 11 10 09   6 5 4 3 2

For permission and ordering information, write to:

CREATIVE

HEALTH CARE

MANAGEMENT

Creative Health Care Management, Inc.
1701 American Blvd. East, Suite 1
Minneapolis, MN 55425

chcm@chcm.com
or call: 800.728.7766 or 952.854.9015

www.chcm.com

This book is dedicated to the memory of my father, Joseph E. Cohen, who taught me the values of courage, perseverance and fair play; and to the memory of my father-in-law, Chester W. Davey, who taught me the values of service and generosity to family and community.

A NOTE TO THE READER

Self-management is an art, not a science. It's a practice. There are no simple answers or magic formulas for success. I do have a distinct point of view, and I present it in a very forthright manner. I may say some things that you flat-out disagree with. That's okay. Through the free marketplace of competing ideas, the truth marches forward.

I hope you will find this book thought-provoking and insightful, but above all practical. My intent is to provide you common sense, down-to-earth advice that you can immediately apply when faced with an on the job challenge.

Ultimately, you will have to find your own way and learn from trial and error what works best for you. If this book helps you in the process, then I have accomplished my objective. Good luck and enjoy the journey!

Michael Henry Cohen

CONTENTS

FOREWORD

The Power of Self Management is a must read for all employees. By applying the principles and strategies outlined in this book, employees can make their jobs easier and more satisfying. They gain control of their work environment and come to understand that "there are no victims, only volunteers. Captivity and powerlessness on the job are almost always self-imposed."

Everyone experiences work frustrations. Mike Cohen asks his readers to take complete responsibility for their own intrinsic motivation, positive attitude and constructive on-the-job conduct. He calls on them to build their own work and service ethics. He helps employees separate *problems* which they can solve from *realities* that are outside anyone's ability to overcome.

My organization has used *The Power of Self Management* and Mike Cohen's expert coaching to effectively address issues between leaders and staff, within and between shifts and work units. With his help, we have learned how to speak with one another in a direct and repectful manner and have been able to more effectively bring our mission and values to life in our daily operations. Problems are being solved at the earliest and most appropriate levels. Employees are practicing assertiveness, while at the same time effectively packaging their ideas so that peers and managers are willing to listen in a non-defensive manner. As a result, the quality of customer service and employee relations has been enhanced.

Every employee and organization will benefit from using *The Power of Self Management* as a practical guide for dealing with everday work problems.

Linda Deering
Chief Operating Officer
Sherman Hospital
Elgin, Illinois

Emotional Intelligence:

The ability to motivate oneself and persist in the face of frustrations; to control impulse and delay gratification; to regulate one's moods and keep distress from swamping the ability to think, empathize and hope.

Daniel Goleman

1

EFFECTIVE RESPONSES TO JOB FRUSTRATIONS

Maintaining positive customer and employee relations within a highly stressful, fast-paced and competitive work environment is a performing art. You're on stage, playing a professional role, and can never break character. Every time that you come into contact with a customer, for example, there is a moment of truth. You are being sized up as if it is an interview. You can never let your guard down.

There are days when you don't feel like "going on." You have a headache or a personal problem, you're upset about a management decision, or your frustration is directed toward another work unit that is not producing in a timely manner. You're tired from lack of sleep or an exhausting schedule. You have to deal with a difficult or toxic personality who is raising havoc with group morale.

How do you effectively respond to these challenges and maintain your professionalism? To be successful, you must possess a high degree of self-esteem and emotional intelligence (Goleman, 2000). These qualities are demonstrated by:

- **Self-Control:** The ability to effectively manage your emotions during pressure-filled, stressful situations. Employees who don't possess this ability are subject to angry outbursts, passive-aggressive responses to conflict, or mood swings.

- **Social Skills and a High Tolerance for Diversity:** The demonstration of empathy, respect, tact and consideration toward co-workers. This quality also includes your ability to appreciate different points of view and work effectively with a variety of cultures, personalities, communication patterns and work styles. Employees who don't demonstrate this skill are judgmental, controlling, self-righteous, arrogant or manipulative.

- **Conscientious Behavior:** The character to take responsibility for your actions and accept the consequences of your decisions. Your willingness to admit a mistake, correct it and take the necessary steps to ensure that it does not happen again. Employees who don't demonstrate conscientious behavior cover up, deny, alibi or minimize the magnitude of the mistake. They are also prone to scapegoat others.

- **Trustworthiness:** The integrity to do the right thing when no one is looking, keep promises, honor commitments, follow through on tasks until successful completion. Employees who don't demonstrate trustworthiness do half-hearted work, cut corners, relax policies and procedures, do just enough to get by and leave work for others to complete.

Your manager is limited in her ability to improve your overall emotional intelligence. Your social skills, for example, were developed during your formative years and built into your character long before you entered the workplace. It is also questionable whether your manager can significantly enhance your:

- **Service Ethic:** Can a manager really motivate you to care? Either you get a kick out of doing something nice for someone or you don't.

- **Pride:** The fundamental belief that if it is a job worth doing, it is worth doing well. The recognition that your primary objective on the job is not to be happy—it is to be successful. Happiness is a by-product of your success. It comes from taking pride in your work and seeing the positive results of your efforts.

- **Attitude:** Your willingness to cast a positive spin on events, and to remain optimistic and constructive while others around you are cynical and prepared to give up. Your ability to focus on the positive aspects of the work environment instead of dwelling on everything that is irritating.

- **Motivation:** Your drive to excel and to continuously improve your performance. Your motivation is intrinsic—your desire to succeed is fueled by passion for the activity in which you are engaged. Your prevailing concern is to be the best you can possibly be and to make a valuable contribution. Hard work and challenging situations are not regarded as a personal sacrifice, because you genuinely want to achieve outstanding results. Doing a good job is highly valued and has meaning in your life.

- **Self-Discipline:** A persistence, resilience and determination to see something through to a satisfactory conclusion. Your willingness to defer immediate gratification to attain long-term objectives.

Because it is very difficult to change someone's integrity or to teach someone common sense, it is critical that your manager select and retain only employees who possess these traits in the first place. In other words, your manager should *hire for attitude and train for skill.* Assuming a new employee has the willingness and capacity to learn, your manager can always enhance the person's technical skills through training. She can increase the person's knowledge through education. Your manager is limited, however, in her ability to change the person's attitude, self-esteem, work and service ethic, intrinsic motivation, or ability to manage stress or conflict.

Human Relations Challenges

If you are like most employees, you enjoy the technical aspects of your job, and you are successful in the execution of your duties. What distresses you is not the *content* of the job, but the *context* in which you perform the work. Your underlying job frustration is caused by a general perception of powerlessness to deal with the human relations challenges and system problems inherent in your work environment. These may include:

- **Organizational Politics**
  Employee comments:
  "I'm having trouble making the system work for me. I can't get the support from 'higher-ups' or secure the resources I need to get my job done."
  "Why can't the people at the top understand what's going on at *our* level? Why doesn't anyone check with us first before making a decision? Why doesn't anyone utilize our expertise? We're on the front lines, making things happen. We're handling the complaints and answering the challenging questions; we know what will work and what won't work. I try telling them, but they won't listen."

- **A Lazy or Incompetent Co-Worker**
  Employee comments:
  "I have to work side by side with a prima donna. She is overbearing and intimidating. She may be technically competent and clinically sound, but her style of addressing problems is creating defensiveness and hostility on the work unit. She's raising havoc with group morale and productivity. I'm trying to resist getting sucked into the conflict, but I don't know what to do."
  "We have this nasty conflict between the day and evening shift. A huge breakdown in communication and cooperation has developed. Customer service is falling through the cracks. The staff is polarized and we can't seem to iron out our differences."

- **Managerial Malpractice**
  Employee comments:
  "My manager is unpredictable. He's subject to extreme mood swings. I never know how he's going to react from

one minute to the next. So I have to be cautious in my communications with him."

"My manager is quick to criticize me when I make a mistake, but rarely, if ever, do I hear a compliment for the good work I do (which is most of the time). Because the only feedback I seem to get is negative, I simply try to avoid him as much as possible."

"Why doesn't my manager do something about this lazy, incompetent co-worker of ours? By doing nothing, he's sending out a signal to the rest of us that the disruptive behavior is acceptable. In the meantime, we all are working harder to compensate for the person's ineptitude, and we resent it bitterly."

- **Inability to Personally Cope**
  Employee comments:
  "I'm having a real difficult time dealing with all the changes going on around here. Every time I turn around someone is being laid off, a program is being dropped, or a new service is being added. We're constantly putting out fires. The pressures are intense, and the stress never seems to let up. While we're short-staffed, management is asking us to work harder and faster. We're beginning to compromise on professional standards to meet the impossible demands. And to add insult to injury, we're being told to smile all the time."

- **Dramatic Shift in Organizational Culture**
  Employee comments:
  "I used to feel as if we were one large family. Everybody looked out for and supported one another. I don't see that any more. Our department is referred to as a 'cost center.' We either produce revenue or represent overhead. It seems the only thing management cares about is the bottom line. Quality is slipping."

- **Abusive People**
  Employee comments:
  "What do you expect me to do when a customer is
  going off on me? Turn the other cheek? Be sensitive
  and understanding when he is verbally abusive? You
  say that the customer is always right. But sometimes
  customers are flat-out wrong. They have unrealistic
  expectations, and they make demands on me that can't
  possibly be met. What do I do then?"

Given these challenges, achieving job success and satisfaction requires common sense, effective communication
and conflict resolution skills. These skills when consistently
practiced add up to self-management and personal accountability—the willingness to take responsibility for your own
thoughts, feelings and actions while creatively adapting to
conditions that are beyond your control.

Your Manager's Role in Facilitating Job Success and Satisfaction

If you maintain a strong work and service ethic and care
about achieving positive outcomes, you want (and deserve)
a manager who holds everyone accountable to high performance standards. By failing to address someone's performance deficiencies or disruptive conduct, your manager
is giving tacit approval for that behavior to continue. *What
your manager accepts is what your manager teaches.* And by accepting mediocrity, your manager demotivates those employees
who want to do the right thing.

To be effective in his role, your manager must practice Tough Love. The *tough* part of the formula is that
your manager should be ever vigilant in pursuit of excel-

lence. He should possess the courage to demand the very best from each employee. He should be willing to stretch people to greater heights of productivity and interpersonal sensitivity.

Your manager must *stand for* something. If he stands for nothing, he is willing to accept anything. And the pursuit of mediocrity is almost always successful. It is important for you to remember that it is not a *right* to work. Nobody is *entitled* to a job. It is a privilege to work within your organization, and with this privilege come specific responsibilities or conditions of employment. These include:

Technical Competence

You can be the nicest person in the world with a winning personality. You can be very well-intentioned and be trying your best to succeed. But, in the last analysis, you must know what you are doing in order to effectively serve the customer and become a fully functioning team member. You can fool *all* of the people *some* of the time. You can fool *some* of the people *all* of the time. But you can't fool all of the people all of the time. Sooner or later, someone is going to call your bluff. Certainly your co-workers know if you are dependent on them to perform certain critical tasks. And while they may cut you some slack for a while, eventually they expect you to become knowledgeable, competent and resourceful.

While everyone is at a different stage on the learning curve, the goal is that every employee should eventually be able to demonstrate state-of-the-art technical skills and be at the cutting edge of his or her profession. Nobody, regardless of age or length of employment, should be permitted to practice OJR (On-the-Job-Retirement). Once you stop learning or are no longer challenged, you get demotivated and habituated.

Therefore, your manager should create a learning culture where everyone is expected to be engaged in continuous quality improvement. In pursuit of this goal, at the end of every performance appraisal, your manager should ask you:

> "This time next year, what will you know that you don't know now, and how will you apply this knowledge or skill to the benefit of the work unit?"

He should create a goal that gets you out of your comfort zone. After establishing this objective, he should discuss existing resources that will facilitate your success in accomplishing the result.

Outstanding Customer Service

Everyone has either internal or external customers. If it is not your job to directly serve the external customer, then it is your job to serve those who do. The goal here is not to just meet the customers' expectations but to exceed— *wow*—them whenever possible. To accomplish this result, you must know the answer to the following questions:

- Who are my customers?

- What are my customers' needs and expectations? What are the criteria by which the customer evaluates me? What does the customer value most in terms of the services that I provide?

- What specifically should I say or do to meet or exceed my customers' expectations?

It is important to recognize that quality of customer service is a perception issue. If customers don't perceive that they have been well served, then by definition, they have not been well served. Quality is whatever the customer says it is.

If enough different customers over a sustained period of time make negative comments about you, they all can't be wrong, crazy or out to get you. If there exists a pattern of negative customer feedback, you must be held accountable for the negative impressions being made. Your manager does not need to directly observe you in action to know that there is a problem. Customer feedback serves as the evidence. It really doesn't matter *how* you attain the negative impressions. The fact that enough credible customers are complaining is sufficient to hold you accountable.

Effective Teamwork

There is no room for a prima donna or lone ranger within your department. You probably don't have enough staff as it is. Therefore, you have a right to expect that every one of your co-workers is cooperative and collaborative within and between job classifications, shifts and work units. At the very least, being an effective team player means:

- Coming prepared for work as schedule requires

- Demonstrating a strong work and service ethic

- Honoring your commitments, keeping your promises and following through on tasks until successful completion

- Talking directly to the person with whom you have a problem
- Avoiding continuous griping, whining or pouting
- Becoming a part of the solution to problems that you identify

Fiscal Responsibility

It is everyone's job to look for ways to make or save money for the work unit or organization. This is demonstrated by:

- Utilizing materials and supplies prudently
- Putting things away
- Locking things up so that they don't disappear
- Taking care of equipment
- Not abusing meal or break times
- Being goal focused and task oriented on paid productive work time
- Identifying creative ways to stay within the budget
- Not badmouthing your work unit or organization to outsiders

It is in your economic self-interest to do all of these things, because without a margin, there is no mission—let alone merit increases, good benefits, or job security.

The *Love* Part of Managerial Tough Love

While your manager must maintain and hold everyone accountable to these high performance standards, he should also care about you as a person. He should attend to your psychosocial needs and do everything possible to set you up for success. All effective managers:

- Model the attitude and behavior expected in employees. They lead by example.

- Provide frequent positive feedback and recognition for achievement. They celebrate individual and team success.

- Maintain high standards for everyone. They don't play favorites.

- Operate from quiet strength. They will *level with you*, but will *not level you*. You know where you stand with them. There are no surprises on a year-end performance appraisal.

- Passionately communicate a vision and set of values and then translate these values into specific, behaviorally concise standards to which everyone is held accountable.

- Train and develop, coach and counsel to facilitate employee success at meeting these standards.

- Listen to employees and involve them in decision-making processes whenever appropriate.

- Share information with employees so that they are not working in a vacuum.

- Remove system barriers that serve as an impediment to employee success. Access permissions and resources from above so that employees can effectively perform their tasks.

- Watch employees' backs. Support them under fire. Defend employees from wrongful accusations or verbally abusive conduct from customers. Serve as an employee ally and politician for employees.

- Facilitate seamless customer service and respectful co-worker relationships through team building within and between work units.

- Maintain a retribution-free communication environment where employees can play the role of loyal devil's advocate without fear of retaliation, providing their critical input is constructive and collaborative.

In short, while your manager is demanding, she is unconditionally respectful of you. She believes in your capacity for growth, and she will do everything in her power to ensure that you live up to your potential. She is such an effective role model and teacher that you don't want to disappoint her.

Your Role in Attaining Job Success and Satisfaction

If you possess the technical and communication skills, creativity and desire to succeed, your manager can channel this energy toward constructive ends consistent with a common vision. But she cannot make you successful. That's *your* responsibility. No matter how inspirational or charismatic your manager may be, she cannot light a fire beneath you unless you already have the spark or will to achieve.

And if your manager lacks some of the leadership qualities described above, as a self-motivated employee you will do a good job anyway. After all, you're not doing a good job for your *manager*. You're doing it for *you*: you take pride in your work. You are about achieving positive outcomes. You are a professional.

If you make yourself dependent upon your manager for your own motivation or success, you place your job effectiveness and satisfaction in a vulnerable position. You become dependent on external forces that are outside your control. Your manager has to like you or approve of your work in order for you to feel secure. You crave the attention and credit you believe you deserve; otherwise you feel neglected. Your manager must be all-knowing, nurturing, attentive and forgiving, or you feel cheated. But your manager can never be everything you want her to be. More important, your manager cannot give you your freedom, self-esteem or security. That's your life's task.

If you desire to work in an organization or for a manager who makes you feel completely safe and protected, the price you pay for it is dependency: You will begin to believe that the "system" should take care of you. Resentment will follow because the organization is not your family and your manager is not your parent. They can't provide you any guarantees for job security. There is no entitlement to lifetime employment. If you really want freedom in your career, the price you pay is personal accountability, knowing that only you are responsible for your career satisfaction and success, and that you always have constructive choices available in response to your work frustrations.

There is no safety in self-management and personal accountability, but taking complete responsibility for your own career is what's necessary to secure success. Of course, independence and autonomy are not to be pursued for their own sake. Freedom without a higher purpose leads to self-absorption and narcissism. And freedom without personal accountability leads to anarchy. As a self-managed person, you claim your autonomy in service to a vision and set of values. You must decide:

> "I'm here to serve, to contribute, to do something that has meaning."

Good managers and co-workers can help you in this endeavor, but they are not the answer to your search for integrity, meaning and value in your career.

To know how other people behave takes
intelligence, but to know oneself takes wisdom.
To manage other people's lives takes strength,
but to manage one's own life takes true power.

Lao Tzu

WHY SELF-MANAGEMENT?

This book focuses on self-management and personal accountability as strategies for successfully dealing with on-the-job stress, change and interpersonal conflict. It is designed to empower you with effective communication skills that will make your job easier, more satisfying and effective. Self-management calls for you to tolerate the common frustrations that are a natural part of your job. When you practice self-management, you accept the limitations of your manager and co-workers, and you learn how to get cooperation from them so that your work is more effective as well as pleasant.

When you practice self-management you demonstrate:

- **Flexibility and adaptability.** You are not paralyzed by change. You are able to adjust to an increasingly fast-paced, highly competitive and constantly changing work environment.

- **Versatility**. You make yourself more valuable when you are willing to learn new skills and apply them to organizational needs. You demonstrate versatility when you accept criticism nondefensively and experiment with new behaviors that lead to personal growth.

- **High tolerance for ambiguity**. In the midst of change and uncertainty, you don't wait for your marching orders. You take the initiative and act affirmatively. You focus on those things that are within your control and do the very best you can, thereby creating your own structure and positive spheres of influence.

- **Respect for differences of opinion**. You effectively manage conflicts, always maintaining integrity and respect for yourself and others. You do this by addressing issues in a collaborative and constructive manner rather than personally attacking a co-worker with whom you are in disagreement.

- **Excitement about new possibilities**. You view change as a challenge and a new opportunity for growth and contribution to the organization. You don't look back to the "good old days" because things will never be the same. As Thomas Wolfe said, "You can't go home again."

- **Realistic expectations**. You understand that there exists no perfect working environment free of frustrations or irritations. Therefore, you take full advantage of the positive aspects of the job, try to improve those things that are within your control to change, and adjust to those things you can't change. You remain flexible in your dealings with customers, your manager and co-workers.

18

Self-Management Is Motivated Primarily by Intrinsic Rewards

Intrinsic motivation encourages you to enjoy work because the activity is enjoyable and meaningful as well as a source of income. When the motivation is essentially extrinsic, the terms of achievement are imposed from outside yourself and are, therefore, outer-directed. As you peruse the chart below, please read each item from left to right as the columns correspond to one another.

When Motivation is Extrinsic or Outer-Directed	*When Motivation is Intrinsic or Self-Directed*
Your desire is fueled by the pursuit of material rewards, praise, or recognition.	Your desire is fueled by passion, pride and a responsible work ethic.
You are preoccupied with the performance of your manager and co-workers, and with organizational politics.	Your primary concern is being the best you can be and making a significant contribution, regardless how others act.
Hard work or challenging situations are resented because of the amount of extra energy and time required to complete tasks.	Hard work or challenging situations are not regarded as a personal sacrifice, because you "own your job" and want to follow through to achieve positive results.
Your focus is on getting credit and on "looking good" in comparison with others.	Your focus is on personal and professional fulfillment. The job itself is highly valued and has meaning in your life.
External success (raises, promotions, job security, prestige, adulation) is largely determined or provided by others.	Intrinsic success (signaled by high self-esteem, pride and enthusiasm) is largely determined by the employee.
The pursuit of external success can easily lead to workaholism and burnout at the expense of personal fulfillment. Work can become all-consuming and exhausting.	The pursuit of intrinsic success usually leads to a healthy balance between personal and work life because you are in touch with your own feelings and values.

Katz, S., Liv, A. (1991). *The success trap*. New York: Dell.

Self-Management Requires High Self-Esteem

Employees with high self-esteem are:

- People who pronounce a self-verdict or self-judgment that indicates, "I have personal power and competence. I intend to work in a fulfilling and personally meaningful way."

- People who are "psychologically" successful within themselves and possess *inner affluence*. Regardless of their level or role within the organization, their underlying belief is that they are living out life's purpose through their own effort and creative will. This inner vision and sense of mission is the primary source of overcoming any obstacle (internal or external). They are able to find something in any assignment that brings them a sense of satisfaction and accomplishment.

- People who possess a moral code of conduct, values, ethics and personal laws to live by. They are not motivated by external injunctions so much as by a belief in themselves and what they stand for.

- People who believe that they are not put on earth to struggle through life. They don't weigh themselves down with the heavy baggage of fear, guilt or other self-defeating thought patterns. They also don't blame others when faced with everyday work frustrations that inhibit their job success or happiness.

- People who are self-disciplined and willing to take the time and effort to get what they want. They solve problems creatively and assertively and act from a base of self-trust. Their self-statements tell them that they have what it takes to figure out what to do when faced with any adversity.

- People who don't hope for someone else to do difficult chores for them or rescue them from the tedious, demanding tasks at hand. They take responsibility to do what needs to be done to accomplish a goal or satisfy a need. They place a great reliance upon themselves, therefore, in determining the course of their work lives.

- People who follow the often slow and difficult path of self-discipline, perseverance and integrity. Regardless of job constraints and limitations, they remain generally enthusiastic, focused and purposeful.

- People who are able to tell others what they need, feel or expect in a plain-spoken, forthright and respectful way. They have successfully faced the challenge of learning how to be treated well.

- People who are able and willing to take risks and move into the unknown. These risks, however, are not taken blindly. They are well planned and typically produce beneficial outcomes. They mentally rehearse and visualize what might happen. They identify their options and then put one hundred percent energy into making the decision or action successful.

- People who allow their weaknesses to be worked on, while their strengths and talents grow into full use. They are in continuous pursuit of self-improvement yet are able to acknowledge and take pride in who they are and what they have already accomplished.

- People who consciously *choose* to do their work and accept the rewards and consequences for this choice. They cultivate self-respect and inner security by ultimately holding themselves responsible for their own job success and happiness.

One thing I know: The only ones among us who will be really happy are those who will have sought and found how to serve.

Albert Schweitzer

THE IMPORTANCE OF A STRONG SERVICE ETHIC

Service as a product is vastly different from the manufacturing of "tangible" products such as automobiles. Cars are manufactured and checked for quality inside and out before they are placed on the showroom floor. There are various checkpoints in the manufacturing process to minimize mistakes. Service as a product, however, is manufactured at the instant of delivery. It has to be right the first time. There is no second chance to create a positive first impression.

Every time a customer comes in contact with you, there is a "moment of truth" in the delivery of your service. With every encounter, you are transacting business and projecting a corporate image. And the sum of every encounter a customer has adds up to her overall evaluation of your quality of service.

It is also important to remember that the customer is motivated by her own particular needs and expectations. She is not necessarily loyal to your organization. Therefore, if you want to gain the customer's voluntary compliance, you must first view her as a consumer who has a choice to willingly accept or reject the services you offer. This requires building a relationship of trust and open communication, of establishing your personal and professional credibility.

The customer's perceptions, right or wrong, are always *real*, and you have to deal with those perceptions as reality. If a customer's expectations of you are unrealistic, you still have to legitimize these expectations, then educate, negotiate or effectively set limits with the customer to get her perceptions in line with "reality". This requires sophisticated communication skills and a nonjudgmental approach to difficult people. After all, your job is not to *judge* the customer. Your job is to serve her. And you can't do both very well at the same time.

For a service-oriented employee, there is no such thing as a "good customer" or a "bad customer." Some people may be more challenging than others, but as soon as you label the customer, you lose the objective psychological distance needed to effectively serve the individual. Service calls for your *unconditional* acceptance of a customer's perceptions or expectations and your willingness to deal with the person as she naturally presents herself to you. It is counterproductive to respond judgmentally based on some preconditioned notion of how the customer *should* be behaving.

You are not going to be judged by your *intent* to do well or by how hard you try. You're going to be evaluated by *results*, by the impact you have on others, and by the impressions you make as a representative of your organization. You can't measure "intent." You can, however, measure results or verify the impact that one person has on another. And in a service-oriented business, your human relations skills often have a greater impact on the customer's perception of quality than your technical or clinical skills do.

Most customers are not experts on the technical aspects of your job. They *assume* that you are technically competent or else you wouldn't be employed within the organization. Your technical expertise is a *given* for them. You can make a technical mistake, and if you catch it in time, the average customer will never know the difference. But all customers are experts on whether they are being treated with empathy, courtesy and respect, regardless of their education, level of income, race or culture.

In health care, for example, patient opinion surveys consistently report the same findings: When a discharged patient feels that employees were unpleasant, she gives the hospital very low marks on the perceived quality of care. She says negative things about the hospital even though she improved physically. On the other hand, when a patient feels that employees were kind and compassionate, she gives the hospital very high marks on the perceived quality of care. She says good things about the hospital even if she did *not* improve physically. These findings confirm that an employee's human relations skills, and an ability to communicate through words and gestures that "I really care for you," are as important as clinical skills.

Health care organizations are engaged in high-stakes competition, and are attempting to project in the public eye a friendly image. When a hospital runs a full-page advertisement in the local newspaper, it doesn't say, "Come to Community Hospital … We Have a Lower *Death Rate* than Memorial Hospital!" Of course not. It's more likely to say, "Come to Memorial Hospital: We Care for You." Hospitals understand that purchases of service are made based upon perceptions of friendliness and convenience as well as on physicians' and employees' technical skills.

The airline industry serves as another example. You would not choose to get on an airplane unless you made two sets of assumptions. The first assumption regards the pilot. You have to believe that he is technically competent. He is not a substance abuser. He does not suffer from an acute state of depression or harbor a secret death wish. He has had a good night's sleep. In short, he is fully capable of navigating the plane.

The second assumption that you make before getting on the airplane is that the ground crew has made the craft airworthy. No defective bolts have been used. All parts have been securely fastened. The engines have been thoroughly checked and are operating properly. You simply want to feel confident that the airplane is completely safe for successful takeoff and landing. You wouldn't endanger your life unless you believed in the technical skills of the airline employees and the safety of the aircraft.

As a consumer, you are not in a position to differentiate one airline carrier from another based upon technical criteria. The airline companies know this. When they run a television commercial, the message to the public is *not* "Fly United Airlines ... we have a better *crash* record than American!" Of course not. Instead, United Airlines has asked potential customers to "Fly the Friendly Skies," attempting to convey a warm and compassionate image. Delta Airlines has countered with "We Love to Fly and It Shows," implying that their employees enjoy their jobs and are eager to please the customer.

In response to the challenge, organizations across the country have instituted extensive customer relations programs for the purpose of making employees more sensitive to the service aspects of their jobs. Improved monitoring and evaluation systems have been established to access and interpret customer perceptions. New recognition strategies have been developed to reward service-oriented employees. Policies and procedures have been audited to determine if they are user-friendly. Team-building programs have been initiated to facilitate improved communication and coordination between departments.

Practicing outstanding customer service is no longer an employee *choice*. It is a condition of employment. There is a bottom-line expectation that effective communications are to be exhibited even under the most stressful situations. This service-management concept is being operationalized through performance appraisals and disciplinary actions. Merit increases and continued employment status hinge on the demonstration of employees' human relations and service-management skills. Customer-focused standards are being built into the evaluation process with the expectation that:

- The employee is able to identify more than one solution or alternative for dealing with resistant customers.

- The employee will invest considerable time developing trust, establishing personal credibility and determining the unique needs of the customer.

- The employee will demonstrate an understanding that the personal relationship she develops with the customer greatly influences her ability to render quality service. Therefore, she must be attentive to the various little things that can be done to convey interest and care.

- The employee will "hustle" for the customer. Hustle is demonstrated by *more* than a quick pace. It is evident in follow-through, enthusiasm and a delivery of service that exceeds (not just meets) customer expectations. Hustle is any action that communicates, "I'm working on your behalf. I will jockey the system, if necessary, to make it work for you. I have your best interests in mind."

- The employee truly gets a kick out of doing something nice for customers, and it shows through both verbal and nonverbal behavior.

The Importance of Effective Employee Relations

The need for displaying outstanding communications is not limited to customer relationships. Managing various conflicts with co-workers, within and between departments, shifts, job classifications and, of course, with your own manager is also an art form requiring sensitive and sophisticated communication skills.

You can't possibly like everyone with whom you work on an equal basis. But whether you are personal friends with a co-worker or not, maintaining an effective working relationship with her will make your job easier, more satisfying and effective. If you don't like someone, you can always say "hello" in the morning, "goodbye" in the afternoon and offer help. You don't have to go home with the person, just spend eight hours in a productive relationship with him. You can be *friendly* without being *friends*. But if this co-worker does something that frustrates your ability to get your job done, you must talk to him about it directly, honestly and respectfully. Instead of raising the person's defensiveness, you must address the issue in a collaborative manner, behind closed doors, within the spirit of confidentiality and noncompetitiveness.

Regardless of the nature or scope of the conflict, you must realize that the organization's mission transcends your turf battles. Your work roles are interdependent: your job begins, ends, and overlaps with his in some fashion. Therefore, it is critical that you cooperate and help each other look good in the eyes of the customer. You may never be the best of pals with this co-worker, and some of your conflicts may never be resolved. But if the conflict can't be resolved, it certainly must be effectively *managed* or customer service will suffer.

Maintaining positive working relationships with co-workers you don't personally like is not a compromise on your integrity, nor does it mean you're being a phony. What it suggests is that you pick your fights with discretion and maintain a functional coexistence with the person. You don't allow a breakdown in the relationship. You play the role of a good "organizational citizen," cooperating with each other as the job dictates.

He who has never learned to follow can never lead.
He who has never learned to obey
can never command.

Aristotle

UNDERSTANDING THE RIGHTS AND RESPONSIBILITIES OF YOUR MANAGER

When you accept a job, you sign your name to an unwritten psychological contract, a covenant of employment that in return for pay and benefits, you agree to:

- Exercise self-control and adhere to standards of professional conduct

- Do whatever it takes within reason to get the job done in a timely and effective manner

- Demonstrate loyalty to your manager, work team and organization

- Legitimize and sanction the right of your manager to schedule time off, assign work, monitor and evaluate performance, coach and discipline, providing these activities are conducted in a legal and ethical manner

You don't have to like your manager personally. But you must respect his position and status within the organization. In the military, for example, when you salute the officer, you are not saluting the *person*. You are saluting the *rank*. It is the role that must be respected regardless of your feelings toward the individual.

Know Your Manager's Rights

Your manager has the right to ask you to do anything and expect that the task will be performed in a timely, effective manner providing:

1. **The expectation is job related:** What you are being asked to do is part of the nature, function and scope of the job. The request is based on business necessity. It is consistent with the organization's mission, vision and values. It is codified within your job description.

2. **The expectation is communicated:** Your manager has shared with you:

   - The tasks to be completed. What specifically you are responsible for.

   - The indicators of success or the standards by which you will be evaluated. A performance standard is a statement that describes how your manager knows when a job is well done or when the outcome meets a targeted goal. Is there a certain way the job should be performed? Are there time frames that must be met? Does a certain degree of quality need to be achieved? What are the specific results to be accomplished?

What policies, procedures, guidelines, protocols, oral traditions, or regulatory mandates must be respected?

- The monitoring method that will be used to evaluate your performance. Will your manager practice MBWA (Management By Wandering Around) to see firsthand how you are performing your tasks? Will he be soliciting customer or co-worker feedback? Will he be reviewing certain documents to assess quality, accuracy and thoroughness?

- How well are you performing relative to your manager's expectations? When and how frequently will you be receiving performance feedback?

- If appropriate, what do you need to do differently in order to meet your manager's expectation?

- What are the consequences if you don't improve your performance?

- What are the resources that exist to facilitate your success (materials; supplies; equipment; staffing; availability of your manager to answer questions, coach, counsel, or assist)?

- Are relationships clear? Do you know who has a right to tell you what to do?

- Do you know what actions you can take independently without informing someone before or after? When must you get permission to do something?

3. **The expectation is reasonable:** The term *reasonable* is subjective and relative. Criteria do exist, however, to determine if your manager's expectation is reasonable. These include:

- Other employees are able to effectively perform the task given the same constraints and limitations.

- Your manager has done this task herself and knows that the expectation is reasonable.

- You are degreed, licensed or certified by a legitimate academic institution. The expectation is in line with professional standards and mandates.

- You have been provided sufficient on-the-job training to perform this task.

- Your manager has removed any system barriers that could serve as an impediment to your success. (You can't be held accountable for an obstacle that is outside your control to overcome.)

4. **The expectation is safe, legal and ethical:** Your manager can't ask you to do something that will put you (or anyone else) at risk physically, legally or ethically. If you ever are asked to do so, you have not only the right, but the responsibility to refuse. You can't use the excuse that "I was just following orders." You are still legally culpable if you knew (or should have known) that what you were being asked to do was wrong.

Know your organization's grievance procedure, corporate compliance plan, chain of command and problem-solving protocols. Know how to access an objective third-party resource who can help you mediate a conflict or interpret your rights and responsibilities.

Meet with your manager on a proactive basis to discuss situational ethics. Identify what potential scenarios may place you at risk, and what should you say or do in order to be supported by your manager.

5. **The expectation is non-discriminatory:** All performance-management decisions must be based on the quality of your work, not personal prejudice. Standards of performance must be consistently applied to everyone. But your manager can't be absolutely fair in the eyes of every employee when she makes a decision or change. In fact, the terms *absolute* and *fair* are at odds with one another. *Absolute* suggests without exception, unconditional, or not to be questioned. *Fair*, on the other hand, is a relative and subjective concept meaning dependent on circumstances or interconnected with a particular situation (not absolute).

Should your manager strive to be consistent and fair in the application of organizational and personnel policies? Yes. But on occasion, she has to make (and is being paid to make) judgment calls based upon her perception of events. It is impossible for her to quantify or objectify these perceptions. However, just because she can't quantify something does not mean it's not real or important. Your manager's perceptions, interpretations and conclusions matter and shouldn't be discounted just because they are inherently subjective. And if you believe those perceptions are unfounded, the burden is on you to effectively change them through word and deed.

One of the most critical determinants of your job success and satisfaction is the working relationship that you establish with your manager. It is as much *your* responsibility as it is your manager's to create and maintain a harmonious and productive working relationship. If you are experiencing difficulty with your manager, it is best to examine what you can do to improve the situation, not what you can get your manager to do. And a large part of successfully "managing your manager" is understanding that she can do only so much to provide for your job satisfaction. She has her administrative tasks to complete and meetings to attend in addition to her employee relations responsibilities. Therefore, you need to maintain realistic expectations regarding her ability to satisfy your needs.

The Nature of Commitments

Every time you accept an assignment, you are, in effect, saying to your manager:

> "Regardless of external forces (foreseen and unforeseen), I will make good on this commitment. You can depend on me."

You are reflecting a clear and strong intent that you will do whatever it takes to produce the desired result.

When you make this agreement, the implication is that you have already assessed the potential roadblocks and limited resources, but you will not be governed by them. You have looked at the external facts and conditions that exist or that may occur in the future, and you have determined that you can deal with whatever comes up. In short, you are creating an island of certainty in an uncertain and unpredictable world. You simply don't agree to do something unless you believe that the circumstances will allow you to honor the commitment, and that you truly intend to follow through to successful completion. If you are unsure about your ability to succeed, you negotiate *up front*, rather than renege on the agreement later.

If you ever agree to do something and later discover that unforeseen conditions prevent you from accomplishing the objective, it is then incumbent upon you to immediately renegotiate the agreement. But this renegotiation cannot be unilateral. The extenuating circumstances should be discussed as soon as they surface, with you and your manager agreeing to a new set of arrangements. If you don't keep her informed of the obstacles which prevent you from honoring the original agreement, and you make excuses after the fact, trust in the relationship breaks down. Your credibility diminishes.

It is your professional responsibility within this working relationship to make informed decisions that are self-promoting and that lead to positive results. It is also your responsibility to recognize all of the constructive choices available to you in response to disagreements with your manager. The choices you make during these occasions will largely determine your job success and satisfaction. The following chapters will discuss in more depth the power of choice in your work life and will describe four specific options available to you when faced with on-the-job frustrations.

Managing Upward

It is critical that you secure a productive and harmonious working relationship with your manager. How well do you "manage your manager?" Use the checklist below to find out:

Do you keep your cool when your manager criticizes your work, providing that the performance feedback is constructive and instructive? Yes__ No__

Comment:

Nobody's perfect. You need feedback to let you know how you're coming across to others and to identify areas for development. Even if you believe your manager is wrong, her perceptions are real and the burden is on you to change those perceptions.

Do you hope and expect your manager will mess up and secretly delight when she does? Yes__ No__

Comment:

Part of your job is to help make your manager look good and to set her up for success. By doing so, your manager will be more willing to facilitate your success and satisfaction on the job or be more forgiving when you make a mistake.

Do you play public win-lose games with your manager? Yes__ No__

Comment:

When you openly go toe-to-toe with the manager, the smart money bets with the manager almost every time. Besides, all disagreements should be aired behind closed doors in the spirit of confidentiality and noncompetitiveness.

Do you badmouth your manager behind her back?

Yes___ No___

Comment:

This practice almost always comes back to haunt you. Remember the time-proven principle, "If you don't have something good to say about someone, it's better not to say anything at all."

Do you expect perfection from your manager?

Yes___ No___

Comment:

If you do, you will be disappointed. Your manager is a human being subject to flaws like everyone else. Maximize her strengths and minimize her weaknesses.

Do you keep your manager informed when something goes wrong?

Yes___ No___

Comment:

Managers hate to trip over problems or find out about them from someone outside the department when you had ample opportunity to inform her about the fact. Cover-ups are often worse than the error itself. Likewise, you can't expect the manager to understand your job constraints and limitations unless you keep open the lines of communication.

Do you sanction and legitimize your manager's right to coach and counsel, make out schedules and assignments, and take corrective actions as necessary?   **Yes__ No__**

Comment:

It's the law of organizational life that everyone is accountable to someone. If you don't personally like or respect your manager as a person, you can at least respect her position and the authority that accompanies it.

Do you empathize with your manager's pressures, job frustrations, insecurities, etc.?   **Yes__ No__**

Comment:

If you are sensitive to your manager's needs and expectations, she will probably be more understanding of yours.

Do you volunteer to do work that goes beyond your job description?   **Yes__ No__**

Comment:

Displaying initiative and going the extra mile shows that you have the best interests of the organization in mind, which casts a positive reflection on you.

Do you insist on having it "your way or no way?"

Yes__ No__

Comment:

One of the principles of job survival is knowing when to "go to the mat" on disagreements and knowing when to "go with the flow." When you constantly demand changes from your manager, you invite defensiveness and resistance. Pick your fights with discretion.

Do you give positive feedback to your manager when deserved?

Yes__ No__

Comment:

Whenever your manager does something that you appreciate, by all means acknowledge it. The positive feedback must be sincere and appropriate, however, or it will be viewed as a cheap gimmick.

Do you utilize your manager as a valued resource to facilitate your success?

Yes__ No__

Comment:

Request your manager's assistance and involvement in areas of her particular interest or expertise. Likewise, demonstrate independence and self-initiative in areas of work in which your manager is not strong.

Do you truly demonstrate self-management?

Yes___ No___

Comment:

The old-fashioned American work ethic of putting in a hard day's work for an honest day's pay still makes sense. When you work hard, the day goes by faster and there is a real sense of pride from doing the best job you can.

Are you using your manager as an excuse for being ineffective or unhappy?

Yes___ No___

Comment:

Sometimes you have to do a good job in spite of your manager. Because of your manager's neglect, you have to get support and recognition from your co-workers. But remember, regardless of your manager's flaws, you are a volunteer and an independent agent. No one has you by ball and chain to your job. No one is captive, victim or powerless unless they choose to be. You always have choices. And not making a choice is a choice.

Do you really understand why you're on the payroll and appreciate the importance of doing a good job?

Yes___ No___

Comment:

Your job, regardless of title or status, is critical to the success of the organization; otherwise the position wouldn't exist. In the last analysis, what you do for a living is not as important as how you do it. Professional success or happiness does not spring from your placement on the organizational chart. It generates from enjoying your work and taking pride in your accomplishments.

How *Not* to Receive Feedback from Your Manager

On the following pages, you will find descriptions of some typical employee responses to negative feedback. Careful consideration of these statements will help you see the world through a manager's eyes.

- "The employee doesn't give me a chance to talk. He argues with everything I have to say even before I have a chance to say it. He interrupts me constantly. I can't finish a sentence."

- "The employee rarely looks at me when I talk to her. I don't know whether I'm being understood or if she's even listening. She doesn't take a personal interest in anything I'm saying. She seems withdrawn and distant. She's unwilling to reveal her own thoughts or get involved in the discussion."

- "The employee actually starts to walk away from me before I'm finished talking to him. When I call him back, he returns acting as if he's doing me a favor. His nonverbal expression communicates, 'Say what you have to say, but make it fast.' He appears to be detached, unconcerned and generally apathetic."

- "The employee interjects humorous remarks even when I'm talking to her about a serious problem. She dismisses the importance of problems by actually laughing them off, saying things like, 'No harm done.' She'll try to sidetrack me and divert my attention to another matter as if the issue I'm addressing doesn't amount to much. What will it take to make her understand I'm serious?"

- "The employee is always making excuses for why he can't accomplish his tasks. If it's not one thing, it's another: The workload is too heavy. There is a lack of time. Someone is not doing their job. There was a shortage of supplies. The temperature is not conducive to quality work. The procedures are cumbersome. He acts as if he is never responsible for the problem. It's always someone or something else that needs to be improved. He shrugs off the notion that co-workers are meeting performance expectations while working under the same conditions."

- "The employee feigns helplessness as if my expectations are always 'out of reach.' If I tell him he must try to work faster to meet production standards, he will say, 'Fine, if that's what you want, I'll do it, but don't blame me if my quality slips.' Or, if I tell him that he is making too many mistakes and to be more careful, his response is 'Fine, if that's what you want, I'll go slower but don't blame me if my production slips.' He acts as if I should not expect him to meet standards of quality and quantity that other employees are able to meet."

- "The employee immediately tries to sidestep the issue of what she did wrong by blaming it on my management style. She suggests that if I would only approach her mistakes in a different (more understanding) fashion, then these errors would not occur. Instead of concentrating on her mistake, I wind up defending myself. If I'm not careful, the employee controls the discussion by coaching and counseling me on how to be a more effective manager."

- "The employee's first response to my constructive criticism of her work is that I don't like her or that I'm picking on her, singling her out while ignoring the mistakes of others. I do deal with co-workers' problems the same way, but I keep this confidential. I think that she is using this as a means of making me feel guilty so I'll go softer on her."

- "As soon as I'm finished giving the employee feedback behind closed doors and in a confidential setting, he goes directly to his co-workers and distorts everything I said. He knows that I won't disclose to anyone what I said in confidence, and I really feel disadvantaged because of my self-imposed silence."

- "The employee never does his mischief in front of me. He always seems to wait until I'm away from the department. Others report his shenanigans to me. When I approach him, his first response is to ask me who snitched. He concentrates on how others don't like him, are out to get him, and how I am always taking their side."

- "The employee takes my negative feedback very personally. She seems crushed by the slightest criticism of her work. She cries. She asks if I want her to resign. I always seem to wind up assuring her that she is a good employee, not to take the criticism too hard, that the problem was not that important anyway. She routinely states that she's trying her best, and that's all I can expect of her, yet the problem keeps recurring."

All of these employee responses signify resistance to the manager's feedback and suggest their mistakes are not likely to be corrected. The employee is too busy defending, justifying, arguing, ignoring or apologizing to hear the manager's feedback clearly and respond to it constructively. A manager expects that you will be receptive to her feedback without necessarily groping for alibis. She expects that you will state your case without theatrics or fanfare, to disagree when necessary, but not become disagreeable. Above all, the manager expects that you *actively listen* to what she has to say and take the appropriate steps to correct the problem.

Notes:

Everything can be taken from a person but the last of human freedoms: The right to choose one's attitude in any given set of circumstances.

Victor Frankl

YOUR POWER OF CHOICE

You're never captive or powerless on the job unless you choose to be. The perception of captivity and powerlessness is self-imposed and is always disabling. Eleanor Roosevelt once observed, "No one can hurt you without your consent." Mahatma Gandhi said, "They cannot take away our self-respect if we do not give it to them." It's your willing permission or consent that helps or hurts you far more than external forces over which you have no control.

Viktor Frankl, a Jewish psychiatrist who was imprisoned in a Nazi concentration camp, illustrates the powerful dimension of choice even under the worst of human circumstances. Frankl's entire family, with the exception of his sister, perished in the camps. He lost *every* material possession and suffered from hunger, cold and brutality. Stripped to his naked existence, he faced potential hourly extermination.

In the concentration camp, every circumstance conspired to make him lose hold of his basic human values. All of the familiar goals in his life were snatched away. But what remained for Frankl was the "last of human freedoms," the ability to "choose one's attitude in a given set of circumstances" (Frankl, 1959, p. 66). Throughout this horrific experience, Frankl chose to maintain a sense of meaning and responsibility in his existence.

Without question, the camps facilitated a strong feeling among the prisoners that fate was their only master and that one must not try to influence it in any way. The temptation was overwhelming to allow the environment to completely dictate one's attitudes and behavior. But within this context, Frankl dared to ask:

> But what about human liberty? Is there no spiritual freedom in regard to behavior and reaction to any given circumstance? Is man no more than a product of many conditional and environmental factors ... be they biological, psychological or sociological? Is man but an accidental product of these? Does man have no choice of action in the face of such circumstances? (1959, p. 65)

One day, naked and alone in a small room, Frankl became acutely aware that apathy could be overcome and irritability suppressed, that he could preserve a vestige of spiritual freedom and independence of mind. The Nazis didn't have the power to take away from him his personal dignity and self-esteem unless he gave it to them. They could do what they wanted with his body, but not control the last of the human freedoms: to choose one's attitude in any given set of circumstances, to choose one's own way. Frankl recalls:

And there were always choices to make. Every day, every hour, offered opportunities to make a decision, a decision which determined whether you would or would not submit to those powers which threatened to rob you of your very self, your inner freedom, which determined whether or not you would become the plaything of circumstances, renouncing freedom and dignity to become molded into the form of the typical inmate....

In the final analysis, it becomes clear that the sort of person the prisoner became was the result of an inner decision and not the result of camp influences alone. Fundamentally, therefore, any person can, even under such circumstances, decide what shall become of him ... mentally or spiritually. He may retain his dignity even in a concentration camp. (1959, p. 66)

Through a series of mental, emotional and moral disciplines, he became an inspiration to those around him, until even some of the prison guards began to admire him for his exhibition of dignity.

If Victor Frankl could identify choices in response to his horrific dilemma, most certainly no one reading this book should feel powerless to deal with her particular work conflicts.

Take Responsibility for Your Attitude

There are many things in life over which we have no control. We can't choose our parents, genetic makeup or upbringing.

We have no control over our birth order or what sign we were born under. We all have limitations, whether a lack of talent, financial resources or physical attributes. We are all on occasion thrust into challenging situations through no fault of our own. But we are always responsible for our *reaction* to what happens to us. In fact, we can never *not* be responsible for our reaction, regardless of circumstances.

Responsibility does not mean blame or guilt. It simply implies that even when provoked, we must ably respond to the situation and account for what we say or do. The freedom to choose without taking responsibility for consequences of our actions leads to a breakdown of civility and order.

Our attitude is a very important choice as it relates to career success and satisfaction. The truth is that anyone, no matter how good the working conditions, can find a reason to have a negative attitude. And anyone, no matter how bad the circumstances, can find a way to maintain a positive attitude. Our attitude is of our own making and largely depends on these influences:

1. **What We Focus On**: Our attitude will likely suffer if we concentrate on everything that is frustrating or unfair and if we take for granted the positive aspects of the working conditions. When we dwell on the negative, we feed it with energy. What we pay attention to only grows stronger.

   The key to happiness is gratitude. All happy people are grateful. Ungrateful people *cannot* be happy. And nothing undermines gratitude more than unwarranted or unmet expectations. The Buddhist teachings are relevant here. If we expect that something desirable will or should definitely happen, then we feel entitled to this thing. This leads to dissatisfaction, because it undermines the most important source of happiness, which is gratitude.

It is assumed that being unhappy leads us to complain. Actually the opposite is true: Complaining helps us become unhappy. Therefore, to improve our overall satisfaction, we should take an inventory of both our personal and work life and express gratitude for all that is good in it (Prager, 1998). Focus on the positive and our attitude will improve.

2. **What We Think When Things Go Bad:** Many of the dissatisfiers at work are irritating, but they are not catastrophes. A catastrophe is the AIDS epidemic in Africa or a hurricane that wipes out a city. What most of us experience when things go wrong at work is frustrating, inconvenient and disappointing, but it is not disastrous. We must place things in proper perspective. Don't become a drama queen or king. Don't make mountains out of molehills or worry about things that have not yet happened (and may not ever happen). This only prevents us from living in the moment, recognizing and taking full advantage of what *is* positive in the work environment.

3. **Whom We Associate With:** If we spend all of our time with someone who is negative and angry, it is very possible that the person's unhappiness will begin to affect our own attitude. Misery likes company, and negativity is very contagious. The disgruntled co-worker *expects* that we join him in his griping and dumping. And if we are too satisfied with our job, there is something wrong with us: We

are naïve. We are in denial. We are apple polishers if we get along too well with management. All of us are judged by the company we keep. Our associations are a reflection of our values. Choose wisely.

4. **Our Expectations:** One definition of conflict is "expectations not met." Therefore, when we are experiencing job-related frustrations, we must examine our expectations. Questions to ask include:

- What do we want, need or expect from this job/department/organization/co-worker?

- Are our expectations realistic given the inherent constraints and limitations (realities) of the workplace?

- If our expectations are reasonable, have we asked for what we want in a clear, concise and constructive manner? Are we packaging our ideas in a way that enables others to listen? Are we actively listening to others so that they are able to talk with us?

- Are we patient, or do we have a need for immediate gratification?

- Have we separated problems (obstacles to job satisfaction that can be resolved) from realities (obstacles that no one can do anything about)?

- If our expectations can't be met here, where can they be met? Are we willing to consider changing our shift, department, organization or career to meet our needs? If not, how can we best accept or adapt to these frustrations and focus on things that *are* within our control?

- Are we willing to concentrate and take full advantage of what is working well within our department?

If working full time, we spend one-half of our waking hours on the job. We probably spend more time with our co-workers than we do our immediate family. It should be a satisfying and fulfilling experience. But the secret to job happiness has less to do with the work environment than with making the right career choices.

The key is to first find a job that we are naturally good at. Work is so much easier when we are engaged in an activity that plays to our strengths. We are more likely to get the recognition we deserve, positive performance evaluations or merit increases when the job is a good match for our God-given talents.

The second key to job satisfaction is to find a job that we truly enjoy. It sometimes doesn't even feel like work when we love what we do. We don't resent the amount of time and effort we invest in the job when we truly care about the results of the activity.

It is difficult to determine which comes first: We generally like what we are good at, and we are good at what we like. It doesn't matter. The secret is to identify our strengths and desires, then find an organization that will pay us to do what comes naturally. The money will follow. And even if the job does not bring us great wealth, we will enjoy *inner affluence* because we are following our bliss.

There will always be aspects of the job that are frustrating and demanding. But we don't mind them so much when we love our work and care about the results of our efforts. To ensure that we have the right job, therefore, we must ask ourselves the following questions:

- What am I naturally good at? What aspects of my job are exceedingly difficult for me? Am I willing to do what it takes to improve?

- What do I enjoy most about my job? What aspects of the work do I enjoy least? Am I willing to perform these least desirable tasks in a pleasant and professional manner?

- What kind of job plays to my strengths?

- What kind of job would actually excite me?

- Where can I make the greatest contribution?

- What do I need to do to prepare for my ideal job? Am I prepared to make the sacrifices necessary to achieve my objective?

We should waste as little time as possible on improving our areas of low competence. Most of our energy should be devoted to cultivating and utilizing our strengths. And no matter how good we are as actors, if we really dislike our job, it shows. No matter how hard we try, people see through our disinterest, disdain or despair:

A labor of love is the work we do not because we are paid but because of the satisfaction it provides. A labor of love cannot be indifferent work, for love cancels out indifference. It is done to the best of our ability because we want to give our best for its own sake. We care so much for what we do that we take the care to do it properly.

When labor is *not* that of love, then how can we talk about it? Is it a labor of hate, is it work without care, is it something done without feeling? Is it utopian to think that we can love all our work? We cannot always find the perfect fit; sometimes the fit is fractured. But it is demeaning to think that we must separate labor and love. For work without love is servitude. (Ginni, p. 223)

Job success and satisfaction are fundamentally interconnected. The only truly effective employees are those working at something they consider important. Ultimately, achievement is the essential precondition for both job satisfaction and self-worth.

To maintain a positive attitude, we must also stop blaming other people or circumstances. We should not wait for a positive change to occur. We should create it by acting in a concrete manner that moves us closer to our objectives. We should experiment with our behavior and examine the results. We must also do less of what doesn't work: If we keep doing what we're doing with negative results, we will keep getting more of the same results. So if we don't like what we're getting, we must change what we're doing.

Finally, let's observe the actions of others we admire most for their job confidence and interpersonal effectiveness, and model their behaviors. People who enjoy a positive attitude and who effectively manage change have these qualities in common:

- They have a strong, healthy self-esteem.

- They take personal responsibility for themselves. They take control over what they think, do, say and feel.

- They face obstacles and setbacks with courage. They accept changes that are outside their control, or they influence the outcome when possible. But they don't play the role of victim.

- They don't put things off. They don't wait around, wondering what to do. They find the answers they need and put themselves into motion. When they catch themselves obsessing over everything that can go wrong, they replace the worry with a plan.

- They get help when needed. They seek out others for support and advice on how to responsibly manage the situation.

- They see unwanted change and conflict as a natural and inherent part of life. They use them as potential catalysts for learning and growing.

- They make the choice to excel in times of difficulty. An accurate description of people who effectively respond to these challenges include such words as:

self-managed	confident
calm	level-headed
optimistic	enthusiastic
determined	empathic
responsible	patient
open-minded	flexible
proactive	resilient
professional	passionate

WHAT DO YOU WANT FROM YOUR JOB?

Please rate the job-related items listed below according to their importance to you.

Job-Related Item	Very Important	Somewhat Important	Unimportant
Accurate and timely feedback			
Appreciation for work well done			
Attention			
Autonomy/control over one's job			
Being treated fairly			
Challenging work			
Clear policies and procedures			
Clear goals			
Flexible job duties			
Flexible schedule			
Good interpersonal relationships			
Good supervision			
Good working conditions			
Interesting work			
Job security			
Leisure time/work-life balance			
More responsibility			
Opportunity for advancement			
Opportunity to learn and grow			
Opportunity to make a difference			
Participation in decisions			
Pay			
Praise/recognition			
Respect			
Support			
Sharing information			
Teamwork/cooperation within and between departments			
Others:			

Initiate a meeting with your manager to discuss which of these items have the most positive impact on your job satisfaction. Be prepared to discuss in specific terms what your expectations are relative to these items. For example, what are the characteristics of a manager who is "supportive?" Do you want her to pitch in when the need exists? Provide you with the resources you need to do your job? Stand behind you when you are unfairly criticized by a customer? Or what form of recognition would be most meaningful to you? Do you want more positive feedback? More thank-yous? More responsibility? What does "more responsibility" look like to you? Would you like to get involved in a special project? Do you have managerial aspirations?

Notes:

Whenever you find yourself inclined to bitterness, it is a sign of emotional failure.

Bertrand Russell

OPTION ONE FOR DEALING WITH WORK CONFLICT: PLAY THE VICTIM ROLE

As hard as we look, we will never be able to find an organization that is free of problems or conflicts. There will always be factors inherent in our job that are unpleasant, frustrating or inhibiting. We have choices in response to these problems. We can approach the situation in a constructive, collaborative manner that facilitates resolution of the difficulty or respond in a way that aggravates and escalates the problem. We can pay attention to what is good and right within the organization and take full advantage of these things. Or we can dwell on the negative and obsess on everything that's wrong, causing us to display an overall negative attitude.

The Passive-Aggressive Employee

Most people do not make a conscious choice to be overly negative, resistant to change and contrary beyond reason.

There is no malicious intent. We don't wake up one morning, look in the mirror and decide, "Today, I'm going to excessively complain, whine and pout." Furthermore, each of us is in the least objective position to see ourselves as others do. We may really believe that we are the only one in the department who cares enough, or is willing to risk enough to complain. We may feel that we are standing up for what's right or fair, and are identifying a real problem that needs looking into. We may perceive ourselves as a "loyal devil's advocate," making an honest attempt to improve the quality of customer or employee relations.

Unfortunately, the passive-aggressive employee's *style* of addressing a problem is so abrasive and induces so much defensiveness that she turns people off. In fact, her communication style calls more attention to itself than the issue being addressed. She can't become an effective change agent or problem solver because her approach gets in the way. She doesn't speak in a manner that makes others willing to listen to her. She also doesn't listen in a manner that makes others willing to talk to her. She prefers grandstanding and ego-tripping over calm dialogue. She prefers accusing and blaming people over collaborating and problem solving.

The passive-aggressive employee frequently displays counterproductive responses to work conflicts:

- She talks to everyone but the person with whom she's having a problem. She goes around the person (backbiting, gossiping) or she will go over the person (tattling).

- If she does choose to confront a co-worker, she unleashes stinging personal criticism in full public view of others, providing no face-saving for the other person.

- If she is upset with you, she will walk right past you in the hallway without acknowledging your presence. No eye contact. No smile. No exchange of pleasantries such as "Hello" or "How are you?"

- In the lounge area, she offers everyone coffee, except you. She gets up from a table when you sit down.

- She won't let you know *why* she's upset. If you ask her to explain what's wrong, she replies: "Nothing! I don't have a problem. Do *you*?"

- She communicates her frustration in nonverbal ways:

  She sighs loudly.

  She mumbles something under her breath.

  She refuses to talk.

  She bangs the desk drawer or slams the office door shut.

- When you inquire as to what's troubling her, she replies:

  "You see, that's exactly the problem. You don't even *know* what you did!"

  "Isn't it obvious?"

  "It won't do any good to talk about. So forget it."

- When she finally does decide to disclose what she's so upset about, an emotional outburst of pent-up aggression is unleashed. The overall tone of her remarks is one of:

  "You're to blame."

  "You started this problem."

  "You are responsible for my negative attitude."

"You're doing this just to get me upset" (assigning malicious intent).

- Because she is so obsessed with who started the problem or who is to blame, she rarely takes responsibility for a problem or offers any solution that includes change on her part. She is too busy judging the motivation or behavior of others and is too overwhelmed by feelings of being victimized to be a constructive team player.

The passive-aggressive employee also has unrealistic expectations of the time it takes to solve a problem. He has an insatiable need for immediate gratification, and as a consequence, advances simplistic, quick-fix remedies to complex issues:

- "Because I want it and deserve it and should have it."

- "*Fair* is however I define it."

- "*Right* is whatever action best serves my self-interest."

Because of his inability to tolerate or adapt to everyday frustrations, he "goes to the mat" on every minor problem. In other words, he doesn't choose his fights with discretion. Every dispute, regardless of magnitude, is the hill he's willing to die on. He is like the child who too often cries "wolf"—when a real problem does arise that deserves serious attention, no one takes him seriously. The manager and co-workers resign themselves to the proposition that nothing will ever make this person happy, so they stop trying. They may feign attention, but few people take this person seriously.

He is a dogmatist. He thinks that he has a corner on the truth, that his way of perceiving a problem is the only way, and that anyone who disagrees with him is either stupid or crazy. He divides co-workers into two camps: Like-minded people are competent, intelligent and morally correct. He rejects anyone who doesn't look, think or act like he does. He views them as inferior, incompetent, ignorant or morally corrupt:

> "If you agree with me, then you're my friend,
> and we can work well together. But if you oppose
> me on this one, you're my enemy, which means I
> can't be friendly or cooperate with you until *you*
> change. So whose side are you on?"

Bored when everyone is cooperating with one another, he likes to stir things up. But he doesn't engage in *open* mischief. He plants the seeds of discontent in private, one-on-one discussions. During department meetings, for example, he is curiously silent when given an opportunity to openly voice concerns or suggest ways to improve the working environment. As soon as the meeting adjourns, however, he engages in animated discussions, lamenting how nothing was accomplished:

- "Do you believe we spent an hour at that meeting? What a total waste of time."

- "This decision will never work!"

- "Did you hear the stupid remark Jane made?"

- "Did you see the look on her face when …?"

- "This is a bad idea. Sounds stupid. No way."

- "Management doesn't know what it's doing."

- "Management doesn't care about us. They're never supportive."

With the instincts of a guerrilla fighter, the passive-aggressive employee becomes a catalyst for intergroup conflict. She thrives on division among workers in different job classifications, between shifts or departments, and in particular between employees and the manager:

- "They always get everything they want."
- "How come we always have to help them? We do our part; why can't they?"
- "We're the only ones who seem to be working around here."
- "Do you think they're worth the money they get paid?"

Nothing the manager does is ever enough. She resists and rejects her manager's leadership by constantly second-guessing decisions and demonstrating a serious inability to accept direction. She has to do things her own way. In fact, she secretly believes that the manager is a burden and a meddler.

She is usually too "streetwise" to actually refuse a management directive and risk losing her job by being insubordinate. For example, she won't say to the manager:

- "I'm not going to listen to you."
- "Take this job and shove it."

Instead, she reluctantly agrees to do what the manager asks, but then does something else. When the manager gets upset that the assignment was not completed as directed, she relies on alibis such as:

- "I got busy and didn't have time to do it" (helplessness).

- "That's not what I heard you say" (misunderstanding).

- "I forgot" (memory lapse).

- "I tried to do what you asked, but it didn't work for me. So I did it my way" (paralysis).

Sometimes the passive-aggressive employee complains and agitates for years. Yet she refuses to quit, preferring to remain unhappy in the same job. When asked why she chooses to stay if things are so bad, her response is:

- "I can't quit because I'll lose my seniority."

- "I can't take a cut in pay."

- "I'm too old to quit and learn a new job."

- "I'm too tired to go back to school."

- "I don't know if I could succeed doing anything else."

- "This job, if nothing else, is secure. I can't take the risk of starting over, being last hired and first fired."

Effectively Responding to the Passive-Aggressive Co-Worker

You can never completely eliminate complaining and gossiping within your work unit. But there are effective responses to employees who have a need to incessantly rumormonger, agitate or complain:

- "Why are you telling *me* this? Have you considered talking directly to the person with whom you have the problem?"

- "This makes me uncomfortable. Let's be loyal to those not present."

- "I wouldn't like being talked about this way. Would you?"

- "How do you know the story you are repeating is even true? Did you see this yourself, or are you just spreading a rumor that could really hurt someone?"

- "I don't know if what you're saying is true or not, but it's certainly not very kind."

- "What you're saying about this person has nothing to do with work. It is really none of our business and we shouldn't be talking about it."

Gossip or rumormongering can be very mean-spirited, and it can destroy someone's reputation. By actively listening, you are inadvertently encouraging it. You should also assume that there is nothing confidential within your work unit. When you say something negative about someone, it will probably get back to him in a distorted fashion. Trust that the relationship might be irreparably damaged.

When a co-worker complains about a particular change or expresses anxiety about a decision that will impact the work unit, consider posing the following questions:

- "What can we do to minimize the chances that our worst fears will be realized? How can we avoid allowing the negative outcome to occur? What can we do to plan for the worst-case scenario?"

- "What can we do to double-check or verify your suspicion?"

- "What can we do to make the change work?"

- "If this problem is outside our control to solve (or if the change is definitely going to happen), what can we do to effectively accept and adjust to this reality?"

- "Let's look at this another way. What are the potential benefits of this change?"

- "This complaining is getting old. We all have choices to make regarding where and for whom we work. What are some alternative choices to the excessive negativity?"

- "If we spend less time complaining or worrying about the change and more time figuring out how we can make it work, we will have better results."

- "I like working here. Even with our problems, it's a lot better than other places where I've worked."

The Aggressive Employee

The aggressive employee, regardless of issue, needs to win, dominate, overcome and control. While an assertive person is unconditionally direct, honest and respectful, the aggressive person is direct and honest, but *disrespectful* toward others' feelings, opinions and belief systems. The aggressor:

- yells
- interrupts

- calls you names

- swears

- violates your personal space

- threatens

- stomps his feet, pounds the table, slams drawers, throws objects

- clenches his fist, flips you the finger, or exhibits other derogatory nonverbal behaviors

The aggressive employee also frequently demonstrates insubordinate behaviors toward the manager. He regularly tests boundaries and limits. If this person perceives a weakness in the manager, he may initiate a challenge just to see how far he can go until the manager pushes back. These behaviors are particularly common if the manager is new to his position, has been promoted from within the work unit and is now supervising his former peers, or is younger than the majority of employees. The aggressive employee may feel a need to demonstrate his bravado by outright defiance and "in your face" conduct.

Examples of an employee's insubordinate behavior include:

- Directly refusing (without an acceptable explanation) to do what is asked of him.

- Turning his back and walking away from the manager, unilaterally disengaging from a discussion.

- Making demeaning statements, such as "That's stupid," or "You're crazy," or "That's the most ridiculous thing I've ever heard."

- Declaring, "This is a bunch of (expletive). I'm not going to take this (expletive). You're full of (expletive)."

- Laughing sarcastically at a manager's comments.

Following one of these episodes, the employee may apologize, feigning regret, but then repeat the same offense. The cycle continues. Or the employee may *say* that he is sorry but then rationalize his actions:

- "You provoked me."

- "You're too sensitive." "You're overacting." "You're taking this personally."

- "I didn't *mean* to offend you." (He wants to be judged by his intent rather than by the direct effect of his behavior.)

- "I was stressed out." "I was having a bad day."

- "This is just the way I am. Deal with it."

- "Okay, I was wrong. But this doesn't warrant a corrective action." (He is unwilling to be held accountable and face the consequences of his behavioral choices.)

Effectively Responding to the Aggressive Employee

If you accept verbal abuse from someone, you're teaching her to give you more abuse. What you permit, you condone and promote. In fact, the only thing a bully understands is appropriate limit setting. You have to stand up for yourself (and your work unit) or she won't respect you:

- "Do not yell at me. Please lower your voice."

- "I was not brought up to be insulted like this. Your language is offensive. You will not swear at me."

- "Are you threatening me? Let's get the manager right now."

- "You're violating my personal space. Please step back."

- "Please don't interrupt me. I listened to what you had to say. Now it's my turn to speak."

- "I don't appreciate a joke that pokes fun at a particular race or ethnic group. It's inappropriate, and it creates a hostile work environment."

The bully might respond:
- "You're not my boss. Don't tell me what to do. Who do you think you are? It's none of your business."

Then your reply could be:

- "I know that I'm not your boss. But I'm your co-worker, and that should count for something. Besides, as professionals, can't we discuss this in a cool, calm manner without getting the manager involved?"

- "That's not just your customer who you verbally abused. He's *our* customer. What you said to him negatively affects the reputation of the work unit. Therefore, this is my business."

Be careful. If you let your guard down, an aggressive employee can provoke you into saying or doing something that you will later regret. When a person is trying to drag you in the mud with his dysfunctional behavior, don't join him; maintain the high ground. Operate from quiet strength. Where appropriate, document the occurrence and seek your manager's counsel.

The Martyr

Martyrs are conflict averse and therefore they avoid confrontation at all costs. They:

- Say "Yes" when they really want to say "No."

- Volunteer for labor-intensive, time-consuming tasks without thinking things through. As a result, they overcommit.

- Resent those co-workers they are helping and get frustrated with themselves for taking on more than they can handle.

Martyrs will do everything expected of them and more. They volunteer to do jobs that others won't or can't do, compensating for their co-workers' shortcomings. At the same time, they complain to significant others about their work load and co-workers who don't do their fair share.

Demonstrating acute passivity, martyrs:

- Walk away from upsetting situations rather than face them directly.

- Apologize even when they have done nothing wrong just to avoid a conflict.

- Feel guilty or responsible when someone disapproves of their actions.

- Ask permission to do things when they already have the authority to act.

- Allow themselves to be repeatedly interrupted.

- Precede their remarks with disqualifying phrases such as:
  "This is only my perception."
  "I may be wrong about this."
  "This may sound stupid."

They also display nonverbal signals that are interpreted by others as weak, vulnerable or self-deprecating such as avoiding eye contact, looking down or to the side when spoken to, or appearing afraid, stunned or about to cry.

Because they are conflict averse, martyrs allow themselves to be willing victims of a co-worker's aggressive or passive-aggressive behavior. Instead of speaking up for themselves and taking a stand, they make rationalizations for their self-imposed impotence:

- "The situation is not that bad. I can live with it."

- "It won't do any good talking to the person. Nothing will change. So what's the point?"

- "I don't know *how* to confront the person. I might say something that I will later regret."

- "I might lose my temper."

- "I might cry."

- "The person won't like me."

- "It could make the situation worse. I could open up a can of worms. Who knows what the reaction will be."

- "The person might plot revenge. I've been burned before. It's not worth the risk."

- "I don't have the right to speak up. I might be overstepping my bounds."

As a result, martyrs defer to others at the expense of their own needs and allow themselves to be taken advantage of. This may lead to depression, withdrawal (escape activities), pent-up anger, displacement of frustrations onto others who are willing to be scapegoats (often family members) and physical symptoms such as headaches and ulcers.

How to Avoid Playing the Martyr Role

Life is too short to spend it griping, feeling angry, captive, victimized and powerless. Leading a life of quiet desperation is a *choice*. You can choose to be unhappy, because you refuse to take responsibility for your own feelings and conduct.

You can't do everything yourself. You must communicate your expectations to co-workers who demonstrate lazy or abusive behaviors. In fact, you have an *obligation* to confront someone whose behavior negatively impacts the quality of performance or reputation of the work unit:

> When we witness an injustice, we have a duty to argue. When we see human beings unjustly used, disrespected, exploited, injured, we have a duty to argue. When we hear unjust statements, we have a duty to not permit the poison to spread unabated....

> We have a duty to argue at home. We have a duty to argue with those we love, with our mates

and our children. We have a duty to argue for ourselves and with ourselves. Yes, we even have a duty to argue with God. Having provided us the skill, I take it that God would be greatly disappointed should it go untested. (Spence, 1996, pp. 16-17)

All that is necessary for the existence of wrongdoing within your organization is that good people do nothing. Problems will never get corrected if employees act as if they see no evil, hear no evil, refuse to speak up or remain afraid to get involved when wrongdoing occurs.

There is no problem so difficult it can't be solved.
If it can't be solved, it's not a problem. It is a reality.
We must accept realities and resolve the problems that
come with them.

Author Unknown

OPTION TWO FOR DEALING WITH WORK CONFLICT: ACCEPT AND ADAPT

Every morning when you awake to your alarm clock, rise from bed, wash, get dressed and come to work, you have made a decision, that at least for today, the advantages outweigh the disadvantages of staying in your present job. As long as you have made this affirmative choice, it behooves you to take full advantage of all positive aspects of your job, adapt to and minimize the negative effect of those problems you can't do anything about, and make an effort to be constructive in all of your work relationships. When you choose to adjust to the imperfections in the workplace, you are following the tenets of the Serenity Prayer:

> "God, let me have the determination to change what I can change, the serenity to accept what I cannot, and the wisdom to know the difference between the two."

Yes, you should have the courage to deal with those work frustrations that can be reduced or eliminated. But like it or not, some things are out of your control to change, and it's better to gracefully accept reality when you cannot change it.

Successful adaptation requires maintaining realistic expectations of your co-workers and your working conditions. Try to overcome problems if, in fact, they are truly resolvable. But first diagnose the problem to determine if it is:

- inevitable

- an inherent condition of the work

- outside your control to change

- outside your manager's control to change

If the problem fits into any one of the categories above, you should make an all-out attempt to:

- Adjust to or accommodate yourself to the situation. After all, why continuously ram your head against a brick wall, trying to move an immovable object, when all this does is give you a headache?

- Minimize the negative impact.

- Count your blessings.

- Focus on things that *are* within your control: your own work and service ethic, intrinsic motivation, positive attitude and constructive conduct.

Remember, you have chosen to work where you do. Economic conditions may limit your options to do something else, but for now it does little good (and much harm) to feel sorry, resent yourself and others around you, and constantly remind yourself how bad things are.

Agonizing about the job's imperfections is almost always self-defeating. You won't like yourself and you will be difficult to work with. Furthermore, your negative attitude will cause others to react defensively toward you. Your behavior influences their behavior, and you unknowingly create a negative self-fulfilling prophecy. Finally, your depression or hostility regarding things outside your ability to change will prevent you from successfully dealing with those work problems that *are* within your control.

Even though you cannot change or control all negative aspects of the working environment, you can choose not to be inordinately jostled about by these problems. You can choose to graciously and peacefully accept the problems and learn to live with them, even though you don't like them. In this way, you don't empower the problems to control you. You place them in proper perspective by taking full advantage of what's good and right within the organization and focusing on those things that are within your sphere of influence.

Successfully adapting to inherent frustrations and limitations in your work life is a mark of personal maturity. Adjusting to those job imperfections that you can't do anything about is also a survival skill. Without this ability, you are likely to take premature stands, inadvertently play the role of the martyr, and set yourself up for frustration and failure.

You should periodically conduct a personal and professional audit to assess your job satisfaction and commitment to the organization that employs you. Here are the critical issues to address as you audit your work:

- **Pay and Benefits:** Do you consider the compensation
  and benefit package fair given the amount of effort
  required to do the job? How does the package
  compare with that of your peers employed within
  the organization when you consider the amount of
  work they have or how well they perform? How does
  the package compare to those of employees in *other*
  organizations or industries engaged in jobs requiring
  comparable education and experience?

- **Work Environment:** Do you work with people you
  like and respect? Do you share a common vision and
  values? Are your recognition needs (praise, status,
  respect) being met? Do you enjoy opportunities for
  professional growth? Are you achieving results that are
  fulfilling? Do you experience the appropriate amount
  of autonomy (freedom, independence and control) over
  your immediate working environment? Is your manager
  responsive to your needs?

- **Job Content:** Do you enjoy the actual tasks in which
  you are engaged? How much effort is required to be
  successful? What are the psychological or physical
  costs involved? Is the effort worth it in relation to
  the rewards? Can you achieve the results that are
  expected? Are these expectations too easily attained,
  thereby not challenging or stimulating? Are the
  expectations too challenging or almost impossible to
  meet?

- **Consequences:** Are you presently on a collision
  course with your manager? How severe are the negative
  consequences if you don't do what's expected? Will you
  receive a marginal performance appraisal? Disciplinary
  action? Discharge? How badly do you want or need this

job? What are your alternatives? What are the risks if
you try something else? What are the risks if you *don't*
try something else?

Once again, you are not captive or victim to your work
situation unless you choose to be. Powerlessness is a self-
imposed condition. If you are miserable in your job or
indignant about your manager's style, understand that no
one has you locked and chained to your present job. As a
self-managed employee, it is your responsibility to make career decisions that are self-promoting and conducive to job
fulfillment.

Morality is simply the attitude we adopt towards people we don't like.

Oscar Wilde

8

OPTION THREE FOR DEALING WITH WORK CONFLICT: BECOME A PROBLEM SOLVER AND CHANGE AGENT

Successfully dealing with work problems requires effective "change-agent" skills. Before you try to address a particular conflict with your manager or co-worker, it is important to understand that you really don't have the power to change anyone. Control over others is an illusion. Ultimately, a person is free to behave any way she chooses, and will do so based upon her own perceived self-interest. You can provide feedback to someone, explaining how her behavior is obstructing the accomplishment of your goals. You can even request that the person change her actions in some way that will make your job more satisfying or effective. You can issue demands, you can plead, cajole, nag, whine or threaten, but until she's ready to change, the behavior will continue.

It is also important to understand that you are not responsible or accountable for another person's behavior. You are always responsible for your own actions, however, and because you have direct control over this area, it is the best place to begin your change efforts. In fact, sometimes your best hope for establishing a positive relationship with a difficult manager or co-worker is to be introspective regarding your own behavior and its effect on the other person. When you demonstrate a willingness to first change yourself, you make it easier for the other person to change in the direction you desire. The following exercise will help you focus on your own areas of control as you attempt to successfully manage a job conflict.

A Self-Management Exercise to Resolve Co-Worker Conflict

The advantage of this conflict-resolution procedure is that it doesn't require direct involvement of your manager or consent of the co-worker. You can do it on your own even without the other person knowing it. It is advantageous, of course, for the manager or co-worker to be a willing partner in the exercise, but this is not necessary to achieve positive results. In fact, your ability to take independent action, regardless of the other's inclination to do likewise, is the value of this exercise.

Step 1: Develop a list of your manager's or co-worker's good qualities.

Recognize and acknowledge what she is doing right. What behaviors do you observe in her that you appreciate and wish to continue? Unfortunately, when a working relationship has gone sour, you have a tendency to overlook (or take for granted) these positive qualities in a person. But you run the risk of extinguishing those behaviors you appreciate in a person when you choose to ignore them. Good behavior needs reinforcement. The person needs to know that you notice when she's doing things to make your job easier, more satisfying, or more effective. Therefore, the first step in resolving the conflict is to develop a laundry list of what the manager or co-worker is doing right.

Step 2: List your bad habits.

Consider what you have done in the past to provoke the other person. Recall her complaints or requests for change on your part. Then develop a laundry list of what you do too much or too little of that probably frustrates your manager or co-worker. If you're not certain how to complete this list, place yourself in the other person's shoes. What would she say you do too much or too little of that frustrates her? It doesn't matter whether the person is right or wrong or whether you do these things intentionally. If she might perceive that you do too much or too little of something, include it in this list.

Step 3: Develop commitments for behavioral change.

Review your list of bad habits (as perceived by your manager or co-worker) and determine which behaviors you are willing to change to improve the working relationship. Write down three things that you're going to do more or less of that will increase your chances for cooperation with the person. Be certain that you commit to things that you are *willing* and *able* to accomplish within a reasonable time frame.

Also, make certain that your three commitments for change will be observable to the manager or co-worker. It's not enough to state, for example, that "I will improve my attitude" or that "I will take more initiative to help you." What will you do specifically to improve your attitude or to demonstrate greater initiative? In other words, describe your commitments in behavioral terms.

Step 4: Initiate a meeting with the manager or co-worker.

After you have completed the previous steps, initiate a confidential meeting with the person to explain the thought processes you've gone through and share your information. It is entirely possible that the person will be just a little bit stunned and suspicious of this whole process. Anticipate and plan for potential resistance, and be determined that regardless of the other's response, you will remain positive. Don't get upset or give up even if the person demonstrates a defensive posture throughout the duration of the meeting. Remember, your manager or co-worker cannot make you act defensively or hostile. You are responsible for your own behavior.

Continuously ask for feedback from the person as you share the information contained in your three lists. Solicit her ideas, check for clear communication, and align yourself with her thoughts. It is particularly important for you not to get angry if she readily agrees with everything you mentioned on your second list (those things you do that bother her). Her agreement simply shows that you were successful in seeing the world through her eyes.

When you divulge your list of commitments, ask the person to accept these behavioral changes as good-faith gestures to improve the working relationship. If necessary, be prepared to develop new commitments based upon the person's feedback. State that you intend to act immediately on these behavioral change commitments, and request that she give you constructive feedback when she observes you are not living up to them.

Your efforts will be wasted if you do not deliver on your commitments to improve the working relationship. Even if the co-worker does not choose to offer commitments of her own to improve the relationship, you have accomplished three things by engaging in this exercise:

- You have become more introspective regarding your behavior and its effect upon the person.

- You have made it easier for the person to change by demonstrating a willingness to first change yourself.

- You have done your part to break the deadlock by acting responsibly. The ball is now in your manager's or co-worker's court to respond in kind.

Examine What You Are Trying to Accomplish

When it becomes necessary to confront a co-worker to address actions that have a negative impact on your job, it is important to check your intentions. If your *real* goal is to threaten, punish, seek revenge, insult, berate, justify and defend your position, or dictate the resolution of the conflict, then there exists little chance of gaining voluntary compliance with your wishes. This approach has a clear "me versus you" orientation. Your energy is directed toward total victory or dominance. You are articulating the problem strictly from your own point of view, rather than defining the issue in terms of mutual needs. The conflict is likely to get personal and ugly. This aggressive approach might serve as a nice catharsis for you, but it will only create defensiveness and polarization, and result in a breakdown of communication and cooperation between you and the other person. Successful conflict management requires the willingness to empathize and talk directly, honestly and respectfully with others. It also requires, when necessary, assertive confrontation and the ability to fight fairly.

Fair-Fighting Techniques

Assertiveness is a collaborative approach to conflict geared toward a "win-win" outcome. When you are assertive, you attempt to depersonalize the conflict; that is, you channel your energies toward solving the problem rather than defeating the other person. You make a real attempt to *understand* the feelings of the other person as opposed to *judging* the other person. As a result, both of you can have your needs met.

When you are assertive, you simply describe the problem from your point of view and the negative effect this problem is having on you. You communicate the problem without attacking the person and you remain constructive regardless of how the other person chooses to behave.

Listed below are specific assertive, fair-fighting strategies which will increase your chances for effectively managing on-the-job conflicts:

1. **Don't expect perfection in others.** Try to maximize people's strengths, minimize their weaknesses and adjust to their imperfections. If you expect perfection in others, you are destined to lead a life of self-righteous, ulcerous indignation. If you expect perfection in yourself, you are destined to lead a life of guilt and frustration.

2. **Choose your fights with discretion.** Some problems aren't worth complaining about. If you gripe about every little thing, you will gain the reputation of "complainer" or "agitator." Furthermore, nobody will take you seriously when a real problem does require someone's attention.

3. **Talk directly to the person with whom you're having the problem.** Sometimes, employees talk to everyone but the person with whom they're having the problem. This creates a breakdown of communication and distrust.

4. **Talk to the person behind closed doors** within the spirit of confidentiality and noncompetitiveness. Don't criticize anyone in public. It only leads to embarrassment and raises a person's defensiveness.

5. **Be cool, calm and collected** when you confront the person with a problem. Don't lead with your emotions; avoid yelling, swearing, interrupting, crying. Don't wave the finger of blame, shame and guilt. Be mindful of the effect that your message (verbal and nonverbal) will have on the other person. Your feedback should make it easier, not harder, for the person to change in the desired direction.

6. **Be issue-oriented**, not personality-oriented. Simply describe the person's behavior (without attacking her) and the negative effects this behavior has on you.

7. **Be open to different interpretations of the same event.** After all, you don't have a corner on the truth. You only have your perceptions of reality. Share your point of view with the person and ask for hers.

8. **Don't sandbag or collect misdeeds,** thereby building up personal resentment for the person. Deal with one issue at a time as it arises. The best feedback is usually immediate feedback as long as you have control over how you're going to approach the person.

9. **Discretion is the better part of valor** and brutal honesty is not always a virtue. Don't say anything to the person that you will later regret. Don't unleash your severest blow. Once you say something in anger, you cannot take it back. The person may forgive you, but may never forget what you said.

10. **Give everyone you deal with an opportunity to save face and keep self-esteem intact.** This is particularly important when you know that you are right on an issue. Give the person "wiggle room" to maneuver rather than backing her into a corner and inviting unnecessary defensiveness.

11. **Know when to terminate the discussion.** If, in the course of a confrontation, you (or the other person) have repeated your best arguments more than once, it is likely that you're "beating a dead

horse" or going around in circles. Agree to disagree for the time being and come back to the discussion later if necessary.

12. **Get a third-party resource** when appropriate to help mediate the conflict. Sometimes you need to talk with someone who has psychological and objective distance to give you advice on how to handle the conflict.

13. **Know when to put the conflict behind you** and "start a new day." Not all work conflicts can be resolved, but as a professional you have to manage these conflicts in an effective manner. Don't get stuck in a conflict mode. There will always be conflicts in a close relationship, but in between the conflicts try to reaffirm the positive aspects of working together.

14. **Don't use personal dislikes as an excuse for a poor working relationship.** Remember, you don't need to like someone on a personal basis in order to work effectively with her. Liking someone is not a precondition for a successful working relationship. Whether you like someone or not, effective communication and cooperation are expected and necessary if you are to be successful in your job.

15. **Don't violate any of the above fair-fighting principles** even if the other person chooses to ignore them. You are always accountable for your own behavior regardless of provocation.

A Department Protocol for Conflict Management

Utilize the following protocol for solving problems with your manager and co-workers.

If you are the offended party:

1. **Speak up.** Find your sense of entitlement to stand up and support yourself. No matter who you are, no matter your title or status, you deserve to be treated with dignity and respect. Your feelings are legitimate and valuable.

2. **Establish a goal for the interaction.** Determine in advance what you want to accomplish when the discussion is completed:

   - "What exactly do I want or need?"

   - "How is this expectation not being met?"

   - "Is my expectation reasonable?"

   - "What do I want the person to start (do more of) or stop (do less of) to satisfy my need?"

3. **Empathize with the person.** Demonstrate an appreciation that the person's perceptions, right or wrong, are real and legitimate to him. A person's perceptions *are* his reality. Anticipate the person's potential for defensiveness, anger, resentment, confusion or feelings of being treated unfairly. Also anticipate the possibility that the person might cry, sulk, withdraw or shout. How will you respond? Be prepared to handle any of these possibilities.

4. **Don't make assumptions about the person's intentions.** You don't always *know* what the other

person is thinking. His intentions are invisible to you. They exist only in the person's heart and mind. And, no matter how real your assumptions are about the person's intentions, they are often incomplete or just plain wrong.

5. **Don't accuse the person of having bad intentions.** Accusing her of trying to hurt, upset or ignore you will naturally make her defensive. More important, you can't *prove* whether this was her motive. It is an unsubstantiated claim that you can't defend.

6. **Intervene early.** Try to solve the problem at the earliest and most informal levels by talking directly to the co-worker *before* you get your manager involved.

7. **Package your message in a constructive manner.** Don't use judgmental terms that will induce defensiveness:

   - "You are being inconsiderate."

   - "You are being lazy."

   - "You are so rude!"

   A more effective way to begin the conversation is

   - "Help me understand why you did that."

   - "My perception is ...."

   - "What you did (describe behavior) had this effect on me: I thought/felt/needed ...."

8. **Involve someone else when needed**. If you anticipate denial or defensiveness, or if you are afraid

of making the situation worse, consider utilizing a third-party resource for assistance in managing the conflict. But don't go to just anyone for assistance. Ensure that the person with whom you seek counsel meets the following criteria:

- The person has good listening skills.

- The person is objective. She has no personal self-interest in the outcome of the conflict.

- The person has credibility. You trust this person to give sound advice. The person has common sense.

- The person will maintain your confidentiality.

- The person is prepared to tell you what you don't necessarily want to hear. The person may empathize with what you are going through, but she may not necessarily agree with how you are handling the situation.

Make certain that you clarify your expectations of the selected third-party resource: Are you using this person as a sounding board? If so, you want the person to understand what happened but do nothing with the information. Do you want the person to offer you advice on how to handle the situation? If yes, ask her to coach you on what to say or even role-play a conversation with your co-worker. Do you want the person to intervene on your behalf, such as bringing both parties together to facilitate a dialogue? Don't expect the third-party resource to do your talking for you. That's *your* job.

If you are confronted by a co-worker:

1. **Listen to what the person has to say.** Don't automatically act defensively:

   - "You are wrong."

   - "Yes, but ...."

   - "That's *not* what happened!"

   - "Who are you to tell me what to do? You're not my boss. I don't have to listen to you!"

2. **Seek to understand before you seek to be understood.** When someone is upset, his fundamental need is to be understood, not agreed with. And when the person is not listening to you, it's not always because he is stubborn. It may be because he doesn't feel heard or he senses that his feelings are not being validated. Therefore, the best way to lower someone's anxiety is to actively listen and ask open-ended, nonjudgmental questions that demonstrate genuine curiosity:

   - "Can you say a little more about how you see this?"

   - "How do you see this situation differently?"

   - "What impact have my actions had on you?"

3. **Empathize and apologize whenever appropriate.**

   - "I'm sorry that you're so upset. This wasn't my intent."

- "I can see this is really hard for you. Thank you for sharing it with me."

- "I am trying to understand this better. Can you tell me again what is it that I said or did that made you so angry?"

- "Can you give me an example of what you're saying I do?"

- "What is it exactly that you would like me to do next time so as to avoid upsetting you?"

4. Verify your understanding by summarizing what you heard the person say.

- "What I hear you telling me is ...."

- "Let me summarize what you're asking of me."

If the responses you get are not entirely clear, keep digging:

- "I'm still unclear about something."

- "What I'm still confused about is ...."

5. Describe the situation from your point of view.

- "My perspective on the event is different. I would like to share with you how I see it and get your response."

- "Let me share with you my perception of what happened."

6. Be prepared to negotiate.

- "Here's what I'm willing to do. Is this acceptable?"

- "Here's what I need from you. Is that okay?"

- "What do you need from me to make it easier to do what I'm asking?"

- "I can do what you're asking of me, but I first need this from you."

7. **If necessary, agree to disagree.** Discuss with the co-worker where you go from here. Not all conflicts can be resolved, but they need to be effectively *managed* or customer service and team morale suffer.

Managing conflict is almost never about getting the facts. It is about different perceptions, judgments and values. It is about what a particular situation means to the co-workers involved. Effective conflict resolution requires assertive communication, active listening, problem solving, achieving closure and moving on (Stone, Patton, Heen and Fisher, 1999).

Empathy: The Key to Effective Conflict Management

Your ability to empathize with people under stressful and strained conditions is critical if you want to successfully manage a conflict. Empathy is more than "walking in the other person's shoes" to see the world from her perspective. If you are a good empathizer, you know a person well enough to accurately predict the responses you will evoke in her based upon your approach. You will feel more secure in the working relationship because you can accurately interpret her attitudes or intentions, perceive situations from her viewpoint and anticipate her behavior in various situations. It is this ability to accurately predict her responses that enables you to avoid unnecessary friction. When disagreements do arise, the use of empathy will help you avoid inadvertent escalation of the conflict.

When you empathize, you:

- Suspend your judgment of the co-worker just long enough to see the world through her eyes.

- Sense the co-worker's confusion, timidity, suspicion, anger or feelings of being treated unfairly as if they were your own.

- Appreciate that no matter how unreasonable, irrational or immoral the co-worker's behavior may appear to you, it is quite reasonable, rational and moral to the co-worker.

- Reflect upon how the co-worker has responded to past behaviors on your part.

- Predict how she might act in the future based upon what you might say or do.

- Choose to act in a manner that you think will evoke the most positive responses in the co-worker.

Empathy requires a nondefensive, nonjudgmental approach to handling differences of opinion. You cannot criticize someone and empathize with her at the same time. These are psychologically opposing states. Empathy is also very strategic. By seeing the world from the other person's point of view, it helps you anticipate and plan for resistance to your ideas. It gives you an opportunity to "package" your ideas in a manner that will be more accepting to her without compromising your basic principles. Besides, you can't completely understand your own position until you fully understand the rationale of your adversary's position. Understanding the other's point of view helps you clarify how or why you have arrived at your position in the first place.

Only secure people are willing and able to empathize. When you empathize, you take the risk of having your perspective changed. You might learn something from the psychological engagement that will alter your thinking. You may not be the same person. Insecure people are unwilling to take this chance. There is safety in certainty, and it is all too easy to dismiss ideas that run contrary to one's belief systems.

We all like to think of ourselves as intelligent, right-thinking and decent, and it is natural to build up psychological defense mechanisms to protect us from an onslaught of opposing ideas. To personally and professionally develop, however, we must be open to other perspectives and risk being transformed. Empathic people take this risk. They recognize that perception is nine-tenths of reality when it comes to interpersonal conflict, and that there is no harm in understanding, if not appreciating, a different point of view. Empathy, after all, is not agreement. It is simply acknowledging that no matter how illogical the other person's perspective is to you, it makes a great deal of sense to her given her set of experiences.

People don't necessarily "see" events the same way. When you are in conflict, therefore, it is helpful to look at things from the other's perspective. Through empathy, you may discover a creative way to resolve or manage the conflict.

Can you see in this picture both the young and elderly woman? It may require an adjustment of *perception* on your part (Covey, 1989).

The *Aikido* Method of Self-Defense: A Strategy for Assertive Confrontation

In Western culture, we are conditioned to respond to force (physical or verbal) by applying equal or greater force in order to win, overcome, control or subdue. This strategy often leads to greater resistance from the aggressor, resulting in a battle over who has greater strength or will power.

In the *Aikido* method of self-defense, you don't automatically go toe-to-toe with your opponent. You don't frontally resist or get in her way. Rather, you use the person's own force or forward momentum against herself. As the *Aikido* master anticipates the moment of physical contact, her competitive advantage is her sense of balance and inward control over her physical and mental processes. She is extremely observant of her opponent's every move. She stays within herself. Instead of directly resisting the force, the *Aikido* master steps aside, deflects the person's energy, gets hold of the opponent, and brings her down in the same direction she was going. The pivotal point in the conflict occurs when the opponent expects resistance and doesn't get it.

The *Aikido* method of self-defense works equally well with verbal assaults, when you are dealing with an angry or demanding person. The following principles are intended to deflect a person's negative energy rather than resist it. The purpose is to establish a win-win rather than a win-lose outcome.

Lessons from *Tao* on Conflict Management

Heider (1986) references Lao Tzu's *Tao Te Ching* regarding effective conflict management strategies:

- Never seek a fight. If it comes to you, yield, step back. It is far better to step back than to overstep yourself. The person who initiates an attack is off-center and easily thrown. Even so, have respect for the attacker. Never surrender your compassion or use your skill to harm another needlessly.

- The greatest martial arts are the gentlest. They allow an attacker the opportunity to fall down.

Gentle interventions, if they are clear, overcome rigid resistances.

- Being open and attentive is more effective than being judgmental. This is because people naturally tend to be good and truthful when they are being received in a good and truthful manner.

- If you are attacked or criticized, react in a way that will shed light on the event. This is a matter of being centered and of knowing that an encounter is a dance and not a threat to your ego or existence.

- Neither avoid nor seek encounters, but be open and when an encounter arises, respond to it while it is still manageable. There is no virtue in delaying until heroic action is needed to set things right. In this way, potentially difficult situations become simple.

- The greatest generals do not rush into every battle.

- Even if harsh interventions succeed brilliantly, there is no cause for celebration. There has been injury. Someone's process has been violated. Later on, the person whose process has been violated may well become less open and more defended. There will be a deeper resistance and possibly even resentment.

- Making people do what you think they ought to do does not lead toward clarity and consciousness. While they may do what you tell them to do at the time, they will cringe inwardly, grow confused, and plot revenge. This is why your victory is actually a failure.

You have brains in your head.

You have feet in your shoes.

You can steer yourself any direction you choose.

You're on your own, and you know what you know.

And You are the one who'll decide where to go.

Dr. Seuss

OPTION FOUR FOR DEALING WITH WORK CONFLICT: SEPARATE FROM JOB

Perhaps the problems that you experience are so serious or all-consuming that they cast a shadow over the positive elements of the job. Perhaps you truly cannot adjust to or tolerate the frustration. The advantages of staying simply don't outweigh the disadvantages. If this is the case, it's time to gracefully separate from your job.

Resigning from a position should be viewed as a last resort, an action to be taken only after exhausting all attempts to resolve the problem. But sometimes quitting makes the most sense, particularly if your negative attitude results in behavior that is harmful to yourself and aggravating to others.

A voluntary resignation from your job is also very practical if you find yourself on a collision course with your manager. Try to avoid at all costs getting fired. Don't place yourself in a position of losing control over your own career. Don't allow your manager to decide for you when to stay or leave. Separate from the job under your own terms and conditions when the time is right for you.

Until you find a better job, play it straight. Do what is expected of you and more. Prove to yourself, co-workers and the manager that you can rise above the differences of opinion, the personality disputes and daily irritations of the job. Demonstrate a willingness and ability to perform your tasks in an above-competent manner. Don't threaten your job security by acting in a way that communicates to others: "I couldn't care less about losing this job." In short, don't burn bridges behind you.

Consider your present job as a link in the chain or a springboard for finding a position that is more suitable to your needs. It is always easier to find a job when you have one than when you don't. Being *forced* out of your job under a cloud of suspicion and hostility will only decrease your chances of landing a more desirable position. Most companies do not look kindly at transferring a troublemaker from one place in the organization to another. And your manager always has the power to give a bad reference, making it difficult for you to land on your feet elsewhere within a reasonable time frame.

If you have determined that sooner or later you will be separating from your present job, make every effort to temporarily adjust to the problems you face. Don't spend a great deal of energy complaining about the situation, making yourself and everyone around you miserable. Don't threaten your manager by delivering an ultimatum (however subtle) that you will quit unless your problems are immediately eliminated. She is likely to call your bluff and the smart money bets on things being resolved in the manager's favor.

Is It Time To Separate?

Examine these questions before you act:

Have you exhausted all reasonable means to resolve the problem or make a satisfactory adjustment to it?   Yes___ No___

Comment:

If you resign over every frustration or irritation that comes your way, you will get the reputation of being a "job-hopper" or "unstable." Future employers look suspiciously at a job application that reflects a series of short-term stints.

Have you decided to quit in a rash moment or when emotionally upset?   Yes___ No___

Comment:

Resignation (oral or written) is often considered an irreversible decision. Think it through before you declare your intent. You may not be able to take it back.

Are you separating when the time and conditions are convenient for you?   Yes___ No___

Comment:

Place yourself in a position where you don't feel pressured to leave, for example, having to quit before you get fired or "beating the manager to the punch." You may need time to make your best career move, and you can buy this time by doing a competent job in your present position. Remember, it's easier to land a new job when you currently possess one than when you don't.

Have you looked long and hard at the advantages versus disadvantages of accepting the new job?   Yes__ No__

Comment:

The grass always appears greener in the other pasture, but as you get closer to it, you begin to see the brown spots and weeds. You may not have the same problems in the new job that you currently experience, but it's guaranteed that there will be another set of problems with which to cope. Second, just because another organization wants you (approval is very seductive), it doesn't necessarily mean that taking the position is the best career move. Think it through.

Have you conducted an attitude check?   Yes__ No__

Comment:

Some people seem to quit or get fired from jobs about every year or so. And they never ask themselves the question, "What might I be doing to sabotage my own career?" They are so busy blaming others for their job frustrations, they fail to understand that they are responsible for the situations in which they find themselves. Either they keep selecting jobs that are not a good match for them, or they bring their negative attitude with them wherever they go. In either case, they don't learn from their past experiences and keep repeating the same mistakes.

Perhaps you have already found another job and are working the last weeks in your current position. Are you inadvertently burning your bridges behind you? Yes__ No__

Comment:

You never know how well you will like your future job until you get there. And even if you are highly successful in your new position, there may come a time when you want to return to your current organization in some other capacity. Therefore, make it your number one objective to separate with working relationships intact. Finish strong.

If I am not for myself, then who will be for me?

If I am only for myself, then what am I?

And if not now, when?

Hillel, the Elder

10

A STUDY IN CONFRONTATION: THE NURSE AND THE VERBALLY ABUSIVE PHYSICIAN

A Study in Confrontation

Recently, I conducted a conflict-management workshop for a group of thirty nurses and had just completed a talk on effective fair-fighting techniques, when a participant expressed some doubts regarding the presentation. She said that she wasn't sure the confrontation techniques would be effective for dealing with a particular physician who was well-known for his obnoxious and verbally abusive communications with hospital employees. To reinforce her position, she shared with me this alarming story:

"I was sitting down at the nursing station completing a patient chart. You must understand that this is a very public place. All around me are employees within and outside my department, engaged in a variety of activities, and I am also in full view of many patients and visitors. All of a sudden when I least expect it, 'Dr. Grouch' approaches me and starts yelling at the top of his voice:

"'You stupid idiot! Who in the hell do you think you are, playing doctor, telling my patient that it's OK to get out of bed without checking this out with me first? This is irresponsible, and as far as I'm concerned it shows your total incompetence to take care of my patients. If I had anything to do with it, I'd kick your ass right out of here.'

"He went on like this, hovering over me, talking down to me as if I were a child in need of a lecture, waving his finger in my face, stomping his feet, acting like a tyrant with a temper tantrum."

"What did you do?" I asked. She continued,

"Well, I didn't know what to do. I was caught off guard and stunned that this could be happening to me. I felt embarrassed and humiliated. I was also extremely self-conscious, feeling as if everyone was staring at me waiting to see what I would do. I felt the tears welling up inside of me. I wanted to respond to his accusations, but every time I tried to utter a sound, he interrupted me. I remember thinking to myself that this is so unfair that I should be expected to accept this kind of treatment from a physician. I felt like standing up and telling him what he could do with his opinions, but I didn't want to get into trouble with administration. So I felt immobilized."

"How did you respond?" I asked.

"Well, I couldn't take it anymore. I thought I was going to lose it and say something to him that I would later regret. So I felt the best thing I could do under the circumstances was to get up and walk away from him."

"What did he do?" I asked.

"This made him really crazy. He yelled at the top of his voice: 'Young lady, where do you think you're going? I'm not through talking with you. Don't walk away from me. Get back here right now. Do you hear me?!?'"

"What did you do then?" I asked.

"Well, at this point the tears were really rolling down my cheeks and I was visibly shaken. I didn't want to give him the satisfaction of letting him know he got to me. I just needed to get away from the situation to catch my breath. So I darted through the double doors of our medical surgical unit onto another floor to escape further confrontation."

"What did he do?" I asked.

"He *followed* me! I could hear him stomping and storming behind me yelling at the top of his lungs:

"'Young lady, you can run, but you can't hide. You're going to have to talk with me sooner or later! Get back here!' Of course, now a scene was being created on another floor with people turning their heads wondering what's going on here.

"As I'm scurrying down the hallway trying to get distance between us, I see out of the corner of my eye a walk-in closet door to my left that was ajar. Without another thought, I quickly darted into the closet, shut the door, held the door knob tightly, and remained there in the total dark until I was confident that he had given up and left. When I felt it was safe, I cautiously cracked open the door, looked in both directions to ensure that the coast was clear, ran out of the hospital and went home."

A kind of eerie silence fell over the group. It was a disgusting and depressing story. Before I could say anything, another nurse, clearly angry about what she had just heard, blurted out:

"Dammit! Who does he think he is treating us like that? We don't have to take this. If he ever tried that with me, it would be his last time. I'd set him back on his heels. Let him get a taste of his own medicine. Let him know how it feels to be talked at that way. Two can play this game!"

"Wait a minute," I said. "What we have here is an ugly incident provoked by an unprofessional physician. What he did is an assault to our sensibilities. But the only two responses available to the nurse that I've heard thus far are *flight* (walk away to avoid confrontation) or *fight* (resort to the same tactics as the physician). Fight and flight are the only choices available to animals when caught in the throes of a conflict: Upon sizing up the situation, if an animal instinctively knows it can't win, it runs away to save its hide. If, on the other hand, the animal believes it can overcome the threat, it will counterattack.

"Fortunately, human beings have a third, more creative choice in response to conflict. We can be *assertive.* Assertiveness, however, is not a knee-jerk reaction to a provocative situation. Assertiveness means that you have the choice to respond in a constructive manner, even if the other person is acting irresponsibly. This abusive physician does not have the power over you to dictate how you will respond. Therefore, this doctor can't force you to run away, any more than he can cause you to fly off the handle."

At this time, I shared with the group how physiologist and psychologist Ivan Pavlov, through experiments in classical conditioning, proved that he could accurately predict an animal's behavioral response to certain stimuli. By carefully allocating the rewards and consequences that accompany a particular stimulus, he showed that an animal would respond in a predictable fashion. Therefore, *stimulus directly causes response* in laboratory animals.

Pavlov's Classical Conditioning Model

Stimulus ──────────────⟶ Response

But when dealing with fully functioning human adults, the classical conditioning model for explaining behavior doesn't work. In people, there is an important gap between stimulus and response, and this gap comprises independent will and the freedom of choice. You can decide for yourself how a stimulus is going to affect you. Difficult people and provocative situations will automatically evoke certain emotions in you, like frustration or hurt. But you always have an independent choice as to how you are going to manage these feelings and act on them (Covey, 1989).

Individual Responsibility Model

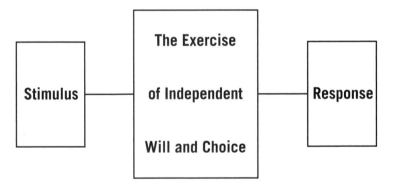

Your independent will and the freedom to choose are what make you unique. You create the meanings. You make sense of the events. You respond to various situations based upon your interpretation of the situation. You have independent will, the choice to act affirmatively and constructively regardless of how someone else is behaving. You have the choice to take responsibility for your actions and to view yourself as an independent agent.

You also have a conscience, a deep inner awareness of right versus wrong, good versus bad, moral versus immoral. If you are grounded by a set of fundamental values and are, regardless of circumstances, ethical in your dealings with people, you are less likely to falter or be compromised when a difficult choice presents itself.

You have your professionalism to consider as well, which is a sense of pride regarding your role and its importance in the organization. You are not just representing yourself on the job. You are representing all those who came before you and you are setting the stage for those who will follow you. You have a responsibility, therefore, to present your profession in the best light possible.

Finally, you have self-esteem, the value or worth you place in yourself. If you feel good about yourself and about what you're doing, you are less likely to be shaken by every criticism or disparaging remark. With self-esteem intact, you are able to respond constructively in conflict even when those around you are behaving destructively. Leo Rosten taught, "It is the weak who are cruel. Softness can only be expected from the strong" (quoted in Phillips, 1991, p. 113). He was not speaking of physical strength but of an internal resolve to believe in oneself, one's capabilities and potential for goodness.

Let's now return to the nurse's story. In the example given, the tyrannical physician did not cause the nurse to walk away. Her choice to escape was largely driven by her internal dialogue or self-talk in the midst of the assault. Her response was, in fact, a direct result of the meaning she placed in the event. As the physician was stamping his feet, yelling at the top of his voice, and speaking in a condescending tone, the nurse was saying to herself: "This shouldn't be happening to me. This is so unfair. This is so embarrassing. Everyone must be staring at me. I feel I'm about to lose it (cry or yell). I really can't trust what I'm about to say next. I need time to think. I need to get away from this situation now."

Given this internal dialogue, it is quite natural for the nurse to flee the scene. But it was the self-talk and not the doctor that caused her response. The nurse did have a choice to interpret the event differently. As the doctor was engaged in his tirade, exhibiting his aberrant behavior, she *could* have been saying to herself:

"He's embarrassing himself. Besides, there's no point getting personally defensive here. He does this to all the nurses. I can rise above this. Now is a great chance to display my professionalism in the face of his unprofessionalism. I'm going to handle this situation with finesse."

If the nurse had engaged in this positive self-talk instead of feeling victimized and powerless, her response would have been different. One assertive response could have been:

"Doctor, I'm as concerned about the patient as you are, and I really do want to discuss this case with you, but not *this way* and not *here* at the nursing station. Let's walk over to the conference room down the hall."

There are no guarantees. The physician might reply: "You're not telling me where to go or how I'm going to talk to you!"

The nurse could then respond: "Doctor, I want to get to the bottom of your complaint. But I will not stand here and be subjected to this kind of language. I believe this discussion is inappropriate, and unless we can talk about the case in a different manner, I'm going to have to leave. Now, would you like to join me in the conference room? If not, we'll have to terminate the discussion right now."

Of course, it takes a nurse with high self-esteem and confidence to respond this way under such stressful circumstances. It also takes preparation. But you can anticipate and plan for such occasions in advance of their occurring, and you can mentally practice your response. After all, this doctor has established a pattern of verbal abuse. He is predictable.

If you say to yourself, "I could never be so cool or calm under pressure like that," you are creating a negative self-fulfilling prophecy that will inhibit any opportunity for growth. A more self-promoting thought would be, "In the past, I have never had it in me to stand up to bullies, but with practice, I can get better."

On the other hand, you might say to yourself, "Assertiveness sounds good in theory. But if a physician (or anyone else) were to verbally assault me that way, I'd have no choice but to give him a taste of his own medicine." This too is a self-fulfilling prophecy. The *thought* is the problem. If you really believe that your behavior is caused by something "out there," by an external stimulus over which you have no control, that there's nothing you can do about it, then you abdicate responsibility. You are reacting to the situation instead of acting on the basis of wise choices.

Epilogue to Physician-Nurse Story

In the conflict-management workshops conducted for all staff nurses within this hospital, participants practiced responding to various conflict-laden situations they encounter with patients, visitors, co-workers and managers. They discussed the advantages and disadvantages of different strategies and reached consensus as to the most effective assertive response to each situation. Participants were also assured by hospital management that they would be fully supported if the time came that these assertive responses would have to be utilized.

Several weeks later, I received feedback from the Vice President of Patient Care Services that nurses were consistently using their newly acquired skills as needed. And, as a result of the assertive response he was receiving from nurses, the verbally abusive physician was showing concrete evidence of positive behavior change. The vice president also said that she had heard from her counterpart at another hospital where the physician had privileges, that he continued to be abusive with nurses at that site. But she was grateful that he had "mellowed out" dramatically in his relationship to her nurses.

This story is instructive in two ways. First, if you accept verbal abuse you are, in effect, reinforcing verbal abuse. What you accept is what you teach. At some point you have to set limits of conduct and abide by them. The example is instructive in another way. The challenge of improving collegial relationships has to be accepted on an individual level. A difficult co-worker is more likely to be abusive with a passive co-worker than he is with an assertive one. The key to effective conflict management, therefore, is to learn constructive assertiveness skills and utilize them even if someone else does not.

Thoughts are like arrows:
Once released, they strike their mark.
Guard them well or one day you may become your
own victim.

American Indian Proverb (Navajo)

UNDERSTANDING YOUR INNER DIALOGUE

For some people, the term "responsibility" is a negatively charged concept associated with feelings of "should" or guilt. But being responsible simply means holding yourself accountable for the results of your decisions or being capable of making moral and rational decisions on your own.

Taking responsibility means that you acknowledge what you bring or contribute to a conflict situation (your input), and that you have an influence on how the situation will be resolved. You can assess your specific responsibility in any conflict by utilizing the Input Box as a model for introspection.

The Input Box contains everything that causes an event to happen. The I-Zone represents everything you bring to the situation: your perception or interpretation of an event, your internal dialogue or self-talk that describes what's happening, and your behavioral response. The They-Zone contains everything in the situation caused by someone or something else: co-workers, fate, circumstance, etc.

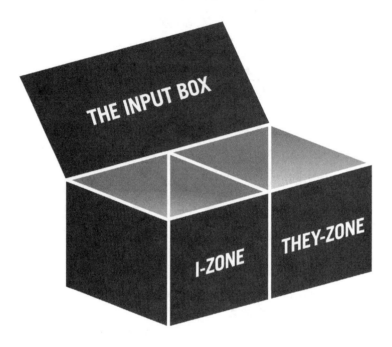

If you are truly self-managed and wish to take responsibility for your own success and happiness, you will focus on the I-Zone in any conflict. The I-Zone is the most critical because it is the only area over which you have direct control. If your intention is to achieve results or become the master of your own fate, you also acknowledge that the *I-Zone* can *never* be *empty*. You choose constructive attitudes and behaviors regardless of how others are behaving. If, on the other hand, your true intention is to assign or avoid blame, it is useful to focus on the They-Zone. By doing so, you absolve yourself of any responsibility. You also create for yourself dependency on outside forces beyond your control. You lose power.

A formula for attaining self-management is to assume that you are always responsible in every situation, even if you don't immediately see how you are. Responsibility is not "blame," "duty" or "obligation." Taking responsibility means you acknowledge your choice to respond with maturity and fairness, regardless of circumstances. As a self-managed, responsible person experiencing conflict, you ask yourself the following fundamental questions:

- "What should be my input to the situation?"

- "What reactions am I evoking in the other person?"

- "Is my true intent to resolve the issue and maintain a positive working relationship for the long term? Or is my true intention to control or get even?"

The willingness to acknowledge input to any situation is a choice, and it is a prerequisite for assuming responsibility. Assuming responsibility is voluntary: You only do it if you want positive results, freedom and power in your life.

The Nurse-Physician story described in the previous chapter illustrates that the way you talk and think about situations in your life affects your sense of responsibility. Your internal dialogue makes you more or less responsible. Words or phrases such as "can't" or "I have to" and "I have no choice but to …" facilitate a self-imposed victim, captive, powerless view, and condition you to see difficult situations as problems instead of opportunities for professional growth. Other erroneous thought patterns include:

- "He makes me feel so mad."

- "She disappoints me."

- "That upsets me."

Each of these statements suggests that someone else is controlling your emotions. It's that person, not you.

In his book *Feeling Good: The New Mood Therapy* (1980), David Beck, MD describes a series of "cognitive distortions" that lead to depression and self-defeating behavior. In each case, it is the individual who facilitates her own disappointments based upon her negative interpretation of the events:

1. All-or-Nothing Thinking

This refers to the tendency to see things in black and white terms. For example, if you are criticized by your manager for a mistake or oversight, you conclude, "Now, I'm a total failure." All-or-nothing thinking forms the basis for perfectionism and causes people to "play it safe," not taking risks for fear of failure.

2. Overgeneralization

This refers to seeing a single negative event as a never-ending pattern of defeat. For example, after the manager's criticism, you say to yourself, "Now I've lost complete credibility in her eyes. She thinks I'm incompetent. I hate to see what my appraisal will look like!"

3. Disqualifying the Positive

This occurs when you reject positive experiences by insisting they "don't really count." In so doing, you ignore or take for granted any positive experiences and only dwell on the imperfections in the environment. For example, you receive a compliment from your manager and you conclude, "She's just being nice," or your reply is "Oh, it was nothing really," thereby disqualifying the positive feedback. This type of response only serves to discourage future compliments and facilitates a negative self-fulfilling prophecy.

4. Jumping to Conclusions

This is when you make a negative interpretation of an event although there are no facts to support the conclusion. For example, your manager passes you in the hallway and fails to smile or say hello. You conclude, "She's ignoring me so she must not like me any more," or "She's mad at me. What did I do wrong?" or "How rude and ignorant she is!" It could be, however, that she is simply absorbed in thought and doesn't notice you. There was no slight or malice intended. Again, the key to a healthy work relationship is in your interpretation and the meaning you place in the event.

5. Magnification (Catastrophizing) or Minimization (Discounting)

This occurs when you inappropriately exaggerate the negative or shrink the positive aspects of any situation. For example, you forget to do something and you say to yourself:

- "My God, I made a mistake, how terrible, how awful! The word will spread like wildfire! My reputation is ruined."

Or, you really accomplished something of significance and you say to yourself,

- "This is really not a big deal. Anyone could have done this."

By magnifying your faults and minimizing your strengths or accomplishments in this way, you set yourself up for low self-esteem.

6. Emotional Reasoning

This occurs when you assume that your negative emotions necessarily reflect the way things really are. You feel it; therefore it must be true. Examples of this include:

- "I feel guilty; therefore, I must have done something bad."

- "I feel overwhelmed or helpless; therefore, my problems must be impossible to solve."

- "I feel inadequate; therefore, I must be worthless."

But thinking it doesn't make it so, unless you act on these feelings, thereby causing them to be validated.

7. "Should" Statements

This occurs when you try to motivate yourself with "shoulds" and "shouldn'ts," as if you have to be psychologically whipped into doing what is right. Likewise, if you direct your "should" or "must" statements toward others, you induce unnecessary defensiveness. In either case, you are imposing some external moral standard on yourself or others.

8. Labeling

This is an extreme form of overgeneralization. Instead of accepting and learning from an error you committed, you attach a disabling label onto yourself:

- "I am a loser."

Or when someone else disappoints and irritates you, you say to yourself,

- "She's a jerk."

- "She's stupid and totally incompetent."

The problem with labeling is that you can't be equated with any one thing you do. Your life is too complex to pin yourself down in such a fashion. Labeling also leads to stereotyping. While it is tempting to reduce someone to a single characteristic, it is also grossly unfair.

9. Personalization

This refers to when you assume blame or guilt for a negative event when there's no basis for doing so. While you are responsible for your own interpretations and behavioral response to any given situation, you're not responsible for someone *else's* attitude or actions. What another person does is ultimately her responsibility. Your actions certainly influence other people, but you cannot control them. Don't give yourself a guilt trip!

If your self-talk reflects any of the above cognitive distortions, recognize that you have a choice to interpret events in a more self-promoting manner. This requires that you continuously challenge the validity of your initial perceptions. These perceptions help create either positive or negative feelings, which in turn, influence your behavioral responses.

Dysfunctional Attitudes Contributing to Job Frustration

Four examples of dysfunctional attitudes that contribute to job frustration:

1. Making Yourself Feel Indispensable

"If I'm not there, the unit will fall apart. People depend on me!"

Comment:

Of course you are valuable, but no one, including yourself, is indispensable. If for some uncontrollable circumstance, you were forced to miss work for a sustained period of time, the unit would survive. When you come to believe that other people could not succeed unless you are ever-present, you assume unnecessary burdens. You need to think about your own needs and if you don't, you will burn yourself out and be unable to provide a valuable service in the long run.

2. Owning Other People's Problems

"When I become aware of someone's troubles, I feel a duty to help them out even if it results in my own inconvenience."

Comment:

This attitude facilitates a hyper-sense of personal responsibility or co-dependency, especially if you focus on meeting the needs of others to the point of self-neglect. Sometimes you can get too personally involved in others' problems. By taking on their burdens or by providing unsolicited advice, you then take responsibility for the outcome of the person's decisions and inadvertently place the proverbial monkey on your shoulders.

3. Doing It All Yourself

"If you want something to be done right, do it yourself!"

Comment:
This attitude facilitates a false sense of independence, making it difficult for you to ask for help, delegate or share responsibility. Your on-the-job survival is contingent upon learning the skills of informal negotiation and delegation. You simply cannot do it all or be all things to all people. You also save much time and lessen aggravation in the long run when you empower others to take responsibility. Delegating is not dumping. If done properly, you develop others' skills, a sense of responsibility and teamwork within the unit.

4. Avoiding Conflict at All Costs

"If I play it smart, I can sidestep controversy and conflicts, thereby making my life more peaceful."

Comment:
Conflict is not bad. Conflict is not good. Conflict just *is*. How you deal with conflict can be very positive or counterproductive. The myth that conflict is inherently negative may cause you to escape from a confrontation that is both necessary and inevitable.

Furthermore, not all conflict can be prevented. You must learn, therefore, how to assertively express your needs and how to set limits when someone is not fighting fairly with you.

Every conflict is an opportunity to test your beliefs, learn from different perspectives and practice assertive self-management. Don't look for unnecessary conflict in your life, but deal with it when it exists. By doing so, you improve the odds of leading a productive and satisfying work life.

Notes:

It is better to light one small candle than to curse the darkness.

Chinese Proverb

YOU ARE NOT ALONE

There are valuable resources within your organization to help you improve your job performance or satisfaction. Below is a checklist of resources offered by many employers. Check the ones that are available to you.

- Manager's availability and willingness to discuss the problem with you if it's addressed in a constructive manner

- Neutral, objective third party (other than manager) to help you sort out the problem on a confidential basis

- Formal grievance procedure

- An Employee Assistance Program advisor

- Career counseling at your local community college

- Continuing education and/or job training opportunities

- Task force or committee membership to identify and solve problems

- Others: _____

In addition to the use of formal organizational resources, it is important to develop an informal support system of friends and professional colleagues. These individuals can serve as a confidential sounding board to help you clarify your work problem and provide you with guidance on how to constructively manage yourself. But ultimately, these people cannot solve the problem for you. Nor should these discussions serve as a substitute for direct, honest and respectful communication with the person with whom *you* are experiencing difficulty. By using the strategies described in this book, the chances are good that you can either effectively resolve the problem or make the necessary attitudinal adjustments that will facilitate your job success and satisfaction.

The power of self-management is great. Yes, you are only one person, but one person can make a difference. You can't do everything, but you can always do something. And what you can do, you should do. Common sense is simply the knack of seeing things as they are and doing things as they ought to be done in a responsible and ethical manner.

Self-management on the job is a commitment to stretch emotionally, intellectually and behaviorally in pursuit of goals that are worthy of accomplishment. The secret to success is to tend unfailingly to an idea, task or a set of values, to have confidence in your abilities, and to apply yourself with all your might to your work. Achievement is not an ethical duty imposed upon someone from above. It is, in the last analysis, a manifestation of your deepest desire that your work will have significance. Every form of job success and happiness is self-motivated. Every great achievement has its source in self-management. Employees who hold themselves personally accountable for positive outcomes don't focus on what others are (or are not) doing. They concentrate on their own opportunities to do what is right and good. And at the end of the day (or career), they leave the campsite cleaner than they found it.

———————————————

Let him who would move the world first move himself.

———————————————

Socrates

SUMMARY AND
SELF ASSESSMENT

Characteristics of a Self-Managed Employee

- Appreciates the work environment yet tries to continuously improve it. Strives toward greater efficiency, to make an operation neater, simpler, faster, safer, more foolproof, with less expense, time and effort.

- Views work as important, even critical, and truly values the opportunity to serve others.

- Enjoys happy endings, good completions.

- Prefers peace and pleasantries over interpersonal and group conflict.

- Demonstrates the capacity to work independently and follow through on tasks.

- Retains a steadiness of purpose in spite of time pressures and limited resources.

- Searches for practical solutions to problems.

- Looks for the latest in new ideas and developments that apply to the workplace.

- Avoids the obvious and advances creative approaches to challenging situations.

- Enjoys situations that stretch skills and imagination.

- Supports a good suggestion in the common interest of the team, regardless who sponsored the idea.

- Works well with a wide range of people, including those with different personalities and work styles.

- Provides constructive criticism without attacking others by "packaging" comments in a sensitive manner.

- Maintains control during frustrating situations.

- Responds to change in an open and flexible manner and works for its success in spite of personal misgivings.

- Brings a touch of professionalism to any job.

Assess Your Prospects for Career Success

As you peruse the chart below, please read each item from left to right as the columns correspond to one another.

Your Chances for Career Success Are Good If:	You Stand a Chance of Losing Your Job If:
You take responsibility for your own success or failure.	You search for alibis when a mistake is made. You don't take responsibility for the problems you face. You get defensive when given feedback on how to improve your work.
You try to establish a win-win relationship with your manager and co-workers. You strive to help them succeed and look good on the job.	You are only concerned about yourself.
You understand your manager's leadership "style," and you try to work effectively within it. You maximize your manager's strengths and minimize her weaknesses. You use your manager as a resource for accomplishing your goals.	You are insensitive to your manager's needs and expectations. You respond only to what's convenient or comfortable for you. You call attention to your manager's limitations and dismiss her strengths. You delight in her failures, and you find subtle ways to embarrass or inconvenience her.
You give your manager the benefit of the doubt when an unpopular decision is made. You check out her reasons and consider them seriously.	You question your manager's intentions and impugn her integrity. You polarize employees from the manager by badmouthing her at every opportunity.
You initiate conversations with your manager to determine how well you are doing on the job.	You choose to remain in doubt regarding the quality of your performance. You allow yourself to wallow in ambiguity or paranoia, not knowing where you stand with your boss.

Your Chances for Career Success Are Good If:	You Stand a Chance of Losing Your Job If:
You take initiative whenever possible. You demonstrate a willingness to "go the extra mile" to get the job done. You "do well what needs doing" without being asked and without constant supervision.	You're reactive and do only what you consider to be within your job scope. You do just enough to get by.
When you have a problem, you ask for what you want or need. You talk directly to those persons who can help.	When you have a problem, you talk to everyone but those individuals who can help. You gossip and backstab.
You are able to adjust to those problems on the job that no one can do anything about. You're selective regarding which issues you address.	You "go to the mat" on everything. You view all problems as critical and demand immediate resolutions.
When in conflict, you maintain self-control. You control others in a private, confidential setting. You discuss differences of opinion in a way that maximizes the chance for reaching an acceptable resolution.	When in conflict, you lead with your emotions and throw caution to the wind. You blurt out whatever comes to mind. You shoot from the hip. You dig in your heels and prepare to fight. You play public win/lose games and provide no face-saving for those with whom you disagree.
You follow through on the commitments you make. You're a person of your word. You work effectively with your manager and co-workers regardless of whether you personally like them.	You bluff and threaten to get your way. You display the attitude; "I don't like her, so I can't (won't) work with her."

A Summary of Conflict Management Strategies

How to Minimize Defensiveness/Hostility in Co-Workers	How to Create Defensiveness/Hostility in Co-Workers
Change one's own behavior first, making it easier for the co-worker to change in the direction you want.	Insist that the co-worker change his attitude or behavior without any change on your part.
Speak to the co-worker as a professional with an equal stake in the improvement of the working relationship.	Come across as superior in thinking or attitude. Talk down to the co-worker.
Be flexible in your position. Allow for adjustment in your thinking and behavior, based upon the co-worker's feedback.	Demonstrate that "my way of seeing the problem is the only way."
Be sensitive to roadblocks the co-worker may face. Initiate offers of assistance to help him overcome them.	Show lack of concern for co-worker's constraints or limitations.
Feedback to the co-worker is direct, honest and constructive.	Try to change the co-worker through deception, manipulation or undermining.
Instead of attacking the co-worker, describe nonjudgmentally what you see or hear him doing. Carefully explain how his actions affect you.	Judge co-worker's intentions, competence or character.

Most Common Irritating Employee Behaviors as Described by Managers

Apathetic and demotivated:

"The employee is practicing 'OJR' (On-the-Job-Retirement). He seems to be "putting in his time" while maintaining a minimally acceptable productivity level. He is passive and unenthusiastic about his work. He doesn't ask questions when unclear about something. He either assumes he knows what to do and makes mistakes, or he sits around waiting for someone to explain it to him. The employee also passes the buck on problems and exhibits the 'It's not my job' syndrome. He is an avid clock-watcher. He demonstrates an inability or an unwillingness to change with the times. He just doesn't seem to care."

Listless:

"The employee has difficulty focusing attention on her work. She doesn't follow instructions or complete tasks such as submitting unfinished reports and returning phone calls. She either procrastinates on activities that should be done immediately, or takes shortcuts on operating procedures to save time."

Unsure:

"The employee has lost confidence in himself which is causing him to make more mistakes. He is having trouble keeping up with the work pace. He is creating a dependency relationship with co-workers and they are beginning to resent having to pick up the slack."

Self-Centered:

"When completed with his own work, the employee doesn't make offers of assistance to others in need of help."

Withdrawn:

"The employee avoids me and acts as if she wants as little to do with me as possible. She rarely says "hello" or "good-bye," much less engage in small talk when the situation permits. She does not consult with me on matters of importance. Indeed, she withholds from me critical information needed to make decisions."

Confrontative:

"The employee becomes quite irritated when I ask him a question or provide direction. He makes it plain that he doesn't like me. He goes over my head with problems when I could be of help. When he does approach me with a problem, he is combative, and he frequently challenges my authority in full view of others."

Subversive:

"The employee seems to be competing for my leadership. I'm suspicious that she's talking behind my back and causing dissension. She makes mountains out of molehills and is raising havoc with group morale."

Unpredictable:

"One day he's fine and everything is sweetness and light. When things are going well for him, he often engages in excessive talking with fellow workers, preventing even the most well-motivated employees from completing their work. But on other days when his mood is foul, watch out! *Anyone* who gets in his way is in trouble."

Not at work as schedule requires:

"The employee's quality of work is first-rate, but her excessive absenteeism is unacceptable. She has established a pattern of frequent one- or two-day absences and is often gone before or after a scheduled day off. Whether she is really sick or not is irrelevant. I need her here on a regular basis so that the work can get done. Her irregular attendance sets a poor example and places a burden on others who must work harder to compensate for her absences." *(Note: Frequent absenteeism and tardiness are the two most documented reasons for disciplining or terminating an employee.)*

Notes:

———————————————

To know and not to do is not to know.

———————————————

Buddha

14

SETTING YOURSELF UP
FOR SUCCESS

Now that you have had an opportunity to review effective self-management strategies for achieving career success, please complete the following Individual Commitment Form.

Individual Commitment Form

One technique that I am going to choose to be more self-managed is:

because:

I will use this behavior whenever:

What do I need help on? Whom can I ask for help? What additional information would be helpful?

What are the biggest barriers I have to guard against, and how can I overcome them?

REFERENCES

Beck, D. (1980). *Feeling good: The new mood therapy.* New York: Signet.

Covey, S. (1989). *The seven habits of highly effective people.* New York: Simon & Schuster.

Frankl, V. (1959). *Man's search for meaning.* Boston: Beacon.

Ginni, A. (2000). *My job, myself: Work and the creation of the modern individual.* New York: Bantam.

Goleman, D. (2000). *Working with emotional intelligence.* New York: Bantam.

Heider, J. (1986). *The Tao of leadership: Leadership strategies for a new age.* New York: Bantam.

Katz, S., Liv, A. (1991). *The success trap.* New York: Dell.

Pavlov, I. P. (1927). *Conditioned reflexes: An investigation of the physiological activity of the cerebral cortex* (translated by G.V. Anrep) London: Oxford University Press.

Phillips, B. (1991). *Powerful thinking for powerful living.* Eugene, Oregon: Harvest House.

Prager, D. (1998). *Happiness is a serious problem.* New York: HarperCollins.

Spence, G. (1996). *How to argue and win every time.* New York: St. Martin's Press.

Stone, D., Patton, B., Heen, S., & Fisher, R. (1999). *Difficult conversations: How to discuss what matters most.* New York: Penguin.

ABOUT MICHAEL HENRY COHEN

Michael H. Cohen is a nationally recognized workshop leader and consultant, specializing in leadership and team development, employee relations, organizational communications, conflict management and customer service. He has taught interpersonal communications, group process, and organizational behavior at Northwestern, Roosevelt and Dominican universities and conducts leadership effectiveness programs for professional associations throughout the United States. Prior to establishing his consulting practice, Michael served as Director of Employee Relations and Development and Vice President, Human Resources at Weiss Memorial Hospital, Chicago, Illinois for 12 years. He holds a Master of Arts in communication studies from Northwestern University and is also the author of *What You Accept is What You Teach: Setting Standards for Employee Accountability* and *On-The-Job Survival: A Guide for Dealing with Everyday Work Problems.*

Information on Michael H. Cohen's management and employee development workshops can be obtained by writing to:

Michael H. Cohen Management Consulting Services
333 N. Euclid • Oak Park, IL 60302
708.386.1968 • canoepress@yahoo.com
www.michaelhcohenconsulting.com

ORDER FORM

1. Call toll-free 800.264.3246 and use your Visa, Mastercard or American Express or a company purchase order

2. Fax your order to: 952.854.1866

3. Mail your order with pre-payment or company purchase order to:

   Creative Health Care Management
   1701 American Blvd East, Suite 1
   IMinneapolis, MN 55425
   Attn: Resources Department

CREATIVE

HEALTH CARE

MANAGEMENT

4. Order Online at: www.chcm.com

Product	Price	Quantity	Subtotal	TOTAL
B519 *The Power of Self Management*	$15.00			
B558 *What You Accept is What You Teach*	$16.00			
B563 *On the Job Survival*	$6.95			
Shipping Costs: 1 book - $6.50, $1 for each additional book. *Call for express rates*				
Order TOTAL				

Need more than one copy? We have quantity discounts available.

Quantity Discounts (Books Only)		
10–49 = *10% off*	50–99 = *20% off*	100 or more = *30% off*

Payment Methods: ☐ Credit Card ☐ Check ☐ Purchase Order PO# _____

Credit Card	Number	Expiration	AVS (3 digits)
Visa / Mastercard / American Express	– – –	/	
Cardholder address (if different from below):	Signature:		

Customer Information	
Name:	
Title:	
Company:	
Address:	
City, State, Zip:	
Daytime Phone:	
Email:	

Satisfaction guarantee: If you are not satisfied with your purchase, simply return the products within 30 days for a full refund.
For a free catalog of all our products, visit www.chcm.com or call 800.264.3246.